At Issue

Biological and Chemical Weapons

Other Books in the At Issue Series:

At Issue

Biological and Chemical Weapons

Amy Francis, Book Editor

GREENHAVEN PRESS
A part of Gale, Cengage Learning

Farmington Hills, Mich • San Francisco • New York • Waterville, Maine
Meriden, Conn • Mason, Ohio • Chicago

Patricia Coryell, *Vice President & Publisher, New Products & GVRL*
Douglas Dentino, *Manager, New Products*
Judy Galens, *Acquisitions Editor*

For more information, contact:
Greenhaven Press
27500 Drake Rd.
Farmington Hills, MI 48331-3535
Or you can visit our Internet site at gale.cengage.com

For product information and technology assistance, contact us at

Gale Customer Support, 1-800-877-4253
For permission to use material from this text or product, submit all requests online at www.cengage.com/permissions

Further permissions questions can be e-mailed to permissionrequest@cengage.com

Articles in Greenhaven Press anthologies are often edited for length to meet page requirements. In addition, original titles of these works are changed to clearly present the main thesis and to explicitly indicate the author's opinion. Every effort is made to ensure that Greenhaven Press accurately reflects the original intent of the authors. Every effort has been made to trace the owners of copyrighted material.

Cover image © Images.com/Corbis.

LIBRARY OF CONGRESS CATALOGING-IN-PUBLICATION DATA

Biological and chemical weapons / Amy Francis, book editor.
 pages cm. -- (At issue)
 Includes bibliographical references and index.
 ISBN 978-0-7377-7153-4 (hardcover) -- ISBN 978-0-7377-7154-1 (pbk.)
 1. Biological weapons. 2. Chemical weapons. 3. Biological weapons--Government policy--United States. 4. Chemical weapons--Government policy--United States. 5. Biological warfare. 6. Chemical warfare. I. Francis, Amy, editor.
 UG447.8.B574 2015
 358'.3482--dc23
                                                          2014030227

Printed in the United States of America
1 2 3 4 5 6 7 18 17 16 15 14

Contents

Introduction

Russia and the United States hold the largest known stockpiles of chemical weapons in the world. While Russia is set to eliminate its stockpile before the end of 2014, the United States estimates it will take until 2023 to completely eliminate the weapons sitting in the two remaining US sites—the Pueblo Chemical Agent-Destruction Pilot Plant in Pueblo, Colorado, and the Blue Grass Chemical Agent-Destruction Pilot Plant in Richmond, Kentucky. According to the Centers for Disease Control and Prevention, together these two sites hold 2,700 tons of chemical agents, including mustard gas and the blistering agent sarin.

There are three main methods of disposing of highly toxic chemical agents: explosion, incineration, and neutralization. Until recently, the method most frequently utilized in the United States was incineration. However, due to environmental concerns, the remaining weapons are set for neutralization, which is more costly and time consuming and is the reason the US government gives for the long delay in disposal.

Even after all these sites are cleaned up, however, a much larger and potentially more dangerous cleanup project will continue for decades into the future. Long before the current methods of exploding, incinerating, and neutralizing chemicals were put into use, unwanted chemical agents were left in trenches, buried in swampy areas, and dumped into the world's oceans. Unlike the stockpiles in Kentucky and Colorado, the abandoned chemicals left primarily from World War II are exposed to nature, in unknown locations and in uncertain condition.

Reported by David Zucchino in the *Los Angeles Times*, there are 249 sites in US states and territories where chemical weapons remain. The largest of these sites is at the Redstone Army base in northern Alabama. Zucchino writes of the area,

"Today a toxic stew of some of the most lethal weapons ever devised rests beneath the surface: Nazi mustard, a liquid blister agent. Lewisite, another blister agent. Adamsite, a vomiting agent. And possibly Nazi tabun, a nerve agent. Also buried are containers of white phosphorus, chlorine, smoke bombs, tear gas and incendiary bombs."[1]

Not all the dump sites are in remote areas. Spring Valley, a section of the District of Columbia near the White House where American University now stands, was once a chemical weapons research and test center. According to information on the US Environmental Protection Agency website, in 1993 a utility worker unearthed a trench of World War I munitions in the area. Additional excavation found soil contaminated with arsenic at a children's play area on the American University campus as well as on ninety residential properties. Blistering agents, mustard gas, and groundwater contaminated with perchlorate, a hazardous compound made up of chlorine and oxygen, were also discovered in the area. As of May 2014, cleanup is still underway.

The United States isn't the only place where leftover chemicals await discovery and cleanup. *China Daily* reported on May 15, 2014, that an estimated two million gas bombs sit in the waterways of China—all left by the Japanese during World War II. Quoted in the article, Jin Chengmin, curator and researcher at The Museum of War Crime Evidence by Japanese Army Unit 731 in Harbin, Heilongjiang province, said that in addition to the gas bombs, "100 tons of toxic substances were left by the Japanese, who either buried them or dumped them in rivers or waterways that feed 17 provinces and regions. Since 1950, there have been more than 2,000 direct victims."[2]

1. David Zucchino, "Deadly Chemical Weapons, Buried and Lost, Lurk Under U.S. Soil," *Los Angeles Times*, March 21, 2014. http://articles.latimes.com/2014/mar/21/nation/la-na-chemical-weapons-20140322.
2. Quoted in He Na and Han Junhong, "Hidden Dangers, Ruined Lives," *China Daily*, May 15, 2014. http://www.chinadaily.com.cn/2014-05/15/content_17508277.htm.

Enormous amounts of chemical weapons were also dumped into the world's oceans, a practice that was not banned until 1972. The James Martin Center for Nonproliferation Studies (CNS) has mapped out 127 known areas where these chemicals remain. According to information on the CNS website, "In the decades following World War I, and even more so after World War II, at least three major powers disposed of massive quantities of captured, damaged, and obsolete chemical warfare (CW) material by dumping them in the oceans. . . . To demonstrate the quantities involved, after World War II 302,857 tons of CW ammunitions were left over in just Germany and the United Kingdom, most of which were eventually dumped in the oceans."[3]

The storage and use of chemical weapons and the potential for a chemical disaster, either accidental or terrorist, is debated by the authors in the following pages of *At Issue: Biological and Chemical Weapons.*

3. Caroline Ong et al., "Chemical Weapon Munitions Dumped at Sea: An Interactive Map," Center for Nonproliferation Studies, August 6, 2009. www.nonproliferation.org /chemical-weapon-munitions-dumped-at-sea.

1

Biological Weapons Pose a Unique Threat to the United States

Stephen Hummel, Vito Quaranta, and John P. Wiksow

Stephen Hummel is a student at Vanderbilt University and a US Army captain who served in both Iraq and Afghanistan. Vito Quaranta is a professor of cancer biology at Vanderbilt Medical School. John P. Wiksow is the founding director of the Vanderbilt Institute for Integrative Biosystems Research and Education and a professor at Vanderbilt University.

Biohacking, the ability of nonscientists to access biological agents, is a dangerous and relatively new threat to the United States. Biological weapons are uniquely dangerous because they can spread unaided from person to person, and there is a long lag time for transmission between the time of infection and onset of symptoms. The threat of biohackers is credible, and further research, though expensive, must be undertaken to find ways to thwart possible attacks.

This article was first published in the CTC Sentinel *in January 2014. The* CTC Sentinel *is published by the Combating Terrorism Center at the US Military Academy, West Point.*

Biological warfare has existed for centuries, with one of the earliest known examples occurring in 1155 when Emperor Frederick Barbarossa poisoned water wells with human bodies in the siege of Tortona, Italy. In 1972, the Convention on the

Prohibition of the Development, Production, and Stockpiling of Bacteriological (Biological) and Toxin Weapons and their Destruction was signed and adopted by the United Nations Office for Disarmament Affairs for enforcement. The treaty aims to prevent the development of offensive biological weapon (BW) agents and eliminate existing stockpiles; however, it only applies to the 170 nation-states that signed the convention and does not affect the actions of the 23 non-signatory states, such as Chad, Israel and Kazakhstan, or independent groups and individuals that seek to employ such weapons.

The 2001 anthrax letters [letters intentionally laced with spores of the anthrax disease, which is caused by the bacterium Bacillus anthracis, were mailed to victims] in the United States demonstrated that the 1972 BW convention limits only one aspect of the problem. Weapons of mass destruction (WMD), once previously under the sole control of nation-states, now could be maintained and deployed by an individual. In 2010, it was concluded that these letters, which were mailed to political leaders and media outlets across the United States, constituted a terrorist attack and were sent by Dr. Bruce Ivins, a trained microbiologist employed by the U.S. Department of Defense.

Another set of biological attacks occurred in April and May 2013. Two separate ricin [a highly toxic protein] letter attacks were allegedly carried out by individuals who, with little to no scientific experience and support, were able to create a biological agent, albeit one that may not have had the potency of an effective weapon. Compared to the 2001 anthrax letters, the 2013 ricin letters illustrated a transition in BW production from the trained individual to the layman, as it has been alleged that the first set of letters was sent by a karate instructor from Tupelo, Mississippi, and the second set from a part-time actress and housewife from Dallas, Texas, who pleaded guilty to sending the letters in December 2013. These recent incidents demonstrated that a relatively low level of sophistication and technological knowledge were no bar to deployment of a WMD.

Biological agent weapons . . . have the potential to create a runaway uncontrollable event.

The ability of non-scientists to create and deploy a biological weapon highlights the emergence of a new threat, the "biohacker." "Biohacking" is not necessarily malicious and could be as innocent as a beer enthusiast altering yeast to create a better brew. Yet the same technology used by a benign biohacker could easily be transformed into a tool for the disgruntled and disenfranchised to modify existing or emerging biological warfare agents and employ them as bioterrorism. A 2005 *Washington Post* article by Steve Coll and Susan Glasser presciently stated that "one can find on the web how to inject animals, like rats, with pneumonic plague and how to extract microbes from infected blood . . . and how to dry them so that they can be used with an aerosol delivery system, and thus how to make a biological weapon. If this information is readily available to all, is it possible to keep a determined terrorist from getting his hands on it?"

This article argues that the biohacker is a real and existing threat by examining evasive biohacking strategies and limitations of current detection methods. The article finds that more active measures are required to stem the growing, long-term threat of modified BW agents employed by individuals. The biohacker is not only a credible threat, but also one that can be checked through improved detection and by disrupting BW agent delivery methods.

The Danger of Biological Warfare Agents

Biological agent weapons, unlike conventional weapons or other WMD, have the potential to create a runaway uncontrollable event. The damage of a bomb or artillery shell is constrained by the blast radius. The effects of chemical and nuclear WMD dissipate over time, albeit with a broad range of half-lives, environmental diffusivities, and ease of decontamination. In contrast, BW are microorganisms that upon dissemination could proliferate exponentially within a single host, linger, and spread from one host to another. BW, therefore, have the potential to be unbounded in both space and time. The hosts themselves serve as potent amplifiers for the agent. Common to all BW agents is the existence of a lag time between time of infection and onset of symptoms. This lag time or incubation period allows infected individuals to feel healthy and to continue with their lives asymptomatically, which increases the potential for spreading.

The Defense Advanced Research Projects Agency (DARPA) commissioned a JASON [an independent group of scientists which advises the US government] study in 2003 to examine the best means to detect, identify, and mitigate the effects of a biological agent release within the United States. The study emphasized that current technologies and those expected to be developed within the next five years could not achieve a nationwide blanket of biosensors. Instead, sensors that are currently available should be used at critical locations according to a pre-established "playbook." Outside the range of these critical nodes, biosurveillance against a bioterrorism event would be accomplished through medical surveillance. The essential component of such surveillance would be the "American people as a network of 288 million mobile sensors with the capacity to self-report exposures of medical consequence to a broad range of pathogens." As a result of the H1N1 flu pandemic, the 2012 National Strategy for Biosurveillance further reiterated the findings of the JASON report and called for medical biosurveillance to move beyond chemical, biological, radiological and nuclear (CBRN) threats. This expansion increases medical surveillance to examine a "broader range of human, animal, and plant health challenges," in an effort to improve early detection of emerging diseases, pandemics, and other exposures.

Medical biosurveillance, however, has an intrinsic limitation: it is entirely dependent on the self-reporting of symptoms and illnesses, which only occurs after an incubation period. This time lag is the window of opportunity for malicious activity by the biohacker aimed at increasing the damage and spread of BW effects. For example, delayed onset of symptoms and ease of international travel enable an individual from the United States to be anywhere in the world within a few hours of BW exposure, potentially infecting hundreds if not thousands along the way. From the biohacker's point of view, a highly virulent pathogen with a short incubation interval and rapid mortality may not be as desirable as a less virulent one, which would allow the infected individuals to travel greater distances before exhibiting symptoms or dying. A biohacker possesses several strategies to maximize the BW incubation period to evade or alter the medical biosurveillance network.

Technological advances and lowering costs make the biohacker a viable threat.

Strategies of the Biohacker

Many biological warfare agents are naturally occurring around the world or easily derived from plants and could be transformed by biohacking. The advent of modern technologies enables the biohacker to employ one or a multitude of strategies to increase the tactical or strategic effectiveness of a biological agent. The authors distinguish five of these strategies as "Wolf in Sheep's Clothing," "Trojan Horse," "Spoof," "Fake Left," and "Roid Rage."

A "Wolf in Sheep's Clothing" occurs when a biological organism or toxin is modified through genetic engineering so that it can be expressed in an active form but does not present the normal epitopes [specific parts of a protein recognized by the immune system]. In a "Trojan Horse," a biohacker maintains the epitope of a non-threatening agent but re-engineers the active component of the toxin to increase the biological threat without increasing the detectability. The "Spoof" occurs when a benign agent is modified to express epitopes distinctive of a known toxin in order to trigger an unnecessary protective response by the target parties (the local, state, or federal government), while the delivering party (the biohacker) can afford to remain unencumbered. The "Fake Left" is a means to modify through selection or genetic engineering the method of transmission of an organism (for example, one that is typically passed by fluid to an airborne method). Such modification makes it easier to disperse an agent among a target population. The "Roid Rage" strategy aims to potentiate the effects of a common virus by expressing components of a deadly virus, such as expressing Ebola virus RNA sequences into the common flu virus. An infected person would demonstrate symptoms of the flu, hampering early detection and treatment of Ebola and favoring its deadly outcomes.

Any of these strategies could be used separately or in conjunction with one another. These strategies also do not require large or sophisticated laboratories to accomplish. Moreover, at the biohacker's disposal is a plethora of scientific data. For example, an article from a major medical journal published last year on the avian flu virus highlighted the five specific genetic modifications required to transmit the virus from ferret to ferret, a model used since ferrets are susceptible to the same flu viruses as humans. Such information provides a framework for biohackers to implement their strategy.

Defending Against the Biohacker

Improving Detection Methods. Advances in biotechnology and genetic engineering facilitate the modification of more BW

15

agents with increased toxicity, transmissibility, and lethality. Many bioengineering companies around the world now openly sell "all-in-one" kits for researchers to perform recombinant DNA experiments. Such kits are available to the public and provide the ability to modify known bioagents. Technological advances and lowering costs make the biohacker a viable threat, but they also enable counter-bioterrorism through cheaper and more reliable detection and identification systems.

One accessible means to thwart the biohacker is the development of physical, chemical, and biological sensors that reliably detect and identify a biological agent by its mechanism of action. For example, the International Genetically Engineered Machine (iGEM) Foundation supports a yearly competition in which competitors are given a "kit of biological parts" and through their own design are expected to build synthetic "biological systems and operate them in living cells." The innovative goals of the iGEM competition in its 242 laboratories worldwide are to promote biosafety and biosecurity by focusing on therapeutics or toxin detection/identification.

Detecting Host Response. Of the various strategies to detect a toxin, the most straightforward focuses on the specific molecular epitope of the active agent, either through molecular recognition (for example, a distinctive surface protein on the organism), or the detection of genetic material specific to a particular pathogen. Unfortunately, these signals can be very weak early into the infection of an individual, and the organisms themselves may be sequestered from ready observation, as was the case with the AIDS virus. The solution to these problems is to continue to increase the sensitivity and specificity of the detection methods, but this in turn may increase vulnerability to hacking. Since these methods depend heavily on the ability to detect specific epitopes, several of the biohacking strategies listed above could be utilized. An alternative approach is to focus not on the agent itself, but on the host response to the agent. In this case, the host serves as an amplifier that produces a multitude of cellular signaling molecules that can potentially be measured to provide an identifying signature, ideally before the onset of clinical symptoms. The host response does not need to be measured in a person since live cell bioreactors with orthogonal quantitative measurements could provide the identifiable signature. While there is no guarantee that the detailed dynamic host response will be pathogen-specific, early detection of an infection is still beneficial by triggering the administration of a drug, a cytokine [a small protein important in cell signaling], or a combination thereof to block progression of the infection.

In contrast [to the current biological detect-to-treat methods], modern technology makes it possible to move to a detect-to-prevent strategy.

Disrupting Delivery. One intrinsic limitation of biohacking is the delivery system. Microorganisms require either a host or stable laboratory cell culture conditions to survive, but some can be effectively placed in a passive spore state that simplifies transmission. Delivery of biological agents is not trivial. Many biological agents, such as anthrax and ricin, are not transmittable from person to person, hence the delivery of millions of spores over a large area is required. Yet, conventional dispersion through munitions would destroy the spores or toxin. The "weaponization" of pathogens may require a certain level of sophistication, but even a non-weaponized agent can have a significant psychological effect. Agents such as Ebola, which are transmittable from person to person, are relatively unstable outside the host, further complicating delivery. Smallpox is an example of a potential agent that is transmittable from person to person and is stable outside the host, but the potential for infection is limited by the smallpox vaccine. Programs to develop specific vaccines, particularly those for animal-borne disease, could provide additional protection. Through knowledge management of scientific data, it might be possible to impede the development of a stable delivery system for malicious purposes.

Curbing Production. In addition, certain equipment and materials, such as fermenters, incubators, enzymes, and retroviruses, are required to modify agents. Limiting the sale or, at the least, monitoring the sale of such materials would also make it difficult for a biohacker to create a modified biological agent undetected. Some of the technologies are simple enough, however, that they could be adapted from readily available consumer items, and even the more complex biological reagents, such as lenti-viruses and specific cell lines, are readily obtainable through research supply companies. Given these challenges, it is important to maintain a strong national effort in detection and prophylaxis bioagent production equipment and supplies.

Conclusion

Unlike conventional weapons or other WMD forms, biological weapons are difficult to contain. The time period that naturally occurs between release and identification provides an opportunity for the pathogen to spread silently. This time period could increase if the biohacker becomes more skilled at hiding agents or modifying incubation times, causing increased transmission. Current detection methods, such as medical biosurveillance and the Joint Biological Point Detection System, abide by the detect-to-treat mentality: they are passive and geared to react to signs of an outbreak or bioagent deployment. In contrast, modern technology makes it possible to move to a detect-to-prevent strategy. The key to such a strategic leap is to reduce drastically the lag time required to correctly identify the biothreat and respond accordingly.

The paradox of new scientific methods and technology, however, is that they lead not only to new discoveries in terms of medicine, but also provide information that enables the biohacker. In a world accustomed to well-defined toxin epitopes and detector receiver-operator characteristics, the hacking of a toxin can be manifested in many ways; for example, in the presentation of an unexpected epitope that could render an existing detection platform ineffective. The modification of BW agents not only makes their identification difficult, but also may render the known therapeutic methods ineffective.

The 2013 ricin letters, in conjunction with the multitude of low-cost tools and strategies available, highlight that the biohacker is a real and contemporary threat. Combating the capabilities of the biohacker will be neither easy nor inexpensive. Although the biohacker still has significant obstacles of production and dispersion to overcome to effectively devastate a large population, the availability of technology and scientific information makes this an impending danger. Continued research is required to develop identification tools that are in front of the medical biosurveillance lag time. The fiscal costs of biodefense are high for continued research and development, but the risk of not stemming the means of the biohacker is even greater.

Captain Stephen Hummel is an FA52 officer who is currently studying Chemical and Physical Biology at Vanderbilt University as part of the Army's Advance Civil Schooling Program. CPT Hummel previously served in both Iraq and Afghanistan and as the USAREUR CBRN plans officer. Upon graduation from Vanderbilt, CPT Hummel will teach in the Chemistry and Life Science Department at the U.S. Military Academy, West Point.

Vito Quaranta, MD, is a Professor of Cancer Biology, Department of Cancer Biology, Vanderbilt University Medical School, Vanderbilt University, and the Director of the Center for Cancer Systems Biology@Vanderbilt, funded by the National Cancer Institute. He conducts a systems-informed effort to characterize the dynamics of cellular responses to perturbations in the context of anticancer drug discovery.

John P. Wiksow, Ph.D., is the Gordon A. Cain University Professor, A. B. Learned Professor of Living State Physics, and Professor of Biomedical Engineeering, Molecular Physiology and Biophysics, and Physics at Vanderbilt University. He is also the founding Director of the Vanderbilt Institute for Integrative Biosystems Research and Education (VIIBRE), where he is directing a large effort in the development of microfabricated devices and organs-on-chips for systems biology, drug development/toxicology/safety, and biodefense.

Acknowledgment: The viewpoints expressed in this article do not necessarily reflect those of the U.S. Army or the Department of Defense.

2

Bioterrorism: A Dirty Little Threat with Huge Potential Consequences

Larry Bell

Larry Bell is a contributing author to Forbes *in the areas of aerospace, environment, energy, and Second Amendment policy.*

Both during the Korean War (1950–1953) and as the Cold War with the Soviet Union was escalating in the 1950s, the United States ran tests on the development and distribution of biological agents. As a result, the government realized the enormous deadly potential of a biological attack on the United States. In more recent years, biological agents have been acquired by potential terrorists, and the United States must take additional steps to understand this threat and take measures to prevent an attack on US soil.

In the early 1950s the evening of September 19th was simply another pleasant balmy night for the residents of San Francisco, California. The year so far had been a tumultus one for the United States, with a Korean War that would have a final death toll of 33,629 American military casualties together with 1.5 million communists from Mao Zedong's China and the military of the Korean peninsula. Dwight D. Eisenhower was the President of the United States, in Europe the Cold War with the Soviet Union was heating up, and an uprising against the communist government of East Germany was developing.

A national polio epidemic was continuing, and Dr. Jonas Salk was developing the world's first Polio vaccine that he would eventually administer to himself and his family. On the lighter side of events, a charming young Queen Elizabeth II would be crowned Queen of England, and a humble New Zealand beekeeper named Edmund Hillary would perform the first successful ascent of Mount Everest. Texas Instruments had just invented the pocket-sized transistor radio, gasoline cost 20 cents a gallon, and the first color television sets would soon go on sale to the public for the princely sum of $1,175.

Testing Biological Agents

Over in Oakland [California], John Renfield and his wife were preparing their two young daughters for bed. The children were both excited over their father's just announced promise to take them to see Walt Disney's new movie *"Peter Pan"* which was showing the next day at the local afternoon matinee. Consequently, it had taken the couple some coaxing to get their two youngsters quieted down and into bed. After watching a half hour of the "Jackie Gleason Show" the couple retired at 8:30, and were soon fast asleep.

As the Renfield family slept quietly and comfortably snug in their beds, a dark grey converted U.S. Navy minesweeper sailed a perpendicular course two miles off the coast of downtown San Francisco. The small vessel had been modified to pass one hundred and thirty gallons of a special homogenized liquid under pressure through a peculiar circular arrangement of specialized spray nozzles located at the very stern of the ship. As the liquid sprayed into the air, the minesweeper left a two-mile long trail of white vapor against the backdrop of the night. Within a few minutes, the larger droplets in the long white cloud fell back into the ocean leaving only an invisible aerosol of microscopic droplets that were gradually blown over San Francisco by the prevailing onshore breeze.

By three AM, the invisible aerosol particles finally reached the Renfield house as well as the homes of all their neighbors, and as the aerosol passed through the neighborhood, some of the droplets seeped into the homes to equilibrate with the volume of air inside them.

American scientists had developed a liquid spray system to disseminate lethal infections . . . to kill and incapacitate enemy soldiers on the battlefield.

The sleeping Renfield family inhaled thousands of bacterial spores of a harmless test microorganism deep into their lungs. Unknown to the Renfield family, they and most of the 800,000 other residents of San Francisco at the time, had just unknowingly participated in one of the most significant military experiments of the Cold War.

The San Francisco test had its origins during World War II, when the American scientists at Camp (later Fort) Detrick and the English scientists at Porton Down began to perfect the military science of biological warfare in response to Japan's use of biological agents in China. Using a series of aerosol dissemination tests at Area B in Maryland, the American scientists had developed a liquid spray system to disseminate lethal infections such as Anthrax, Tularemia, Psittacosis, and Brucellosis to kill and incapacitate enemy soldiers on the battlefield. Concerned over the possibility that Soviet submarines might one day surface off the coast of the U.S. and employ the same techniques, a series of large-scale open-air vulnerability tests were conducted on several American cities, as well as in the New York subway system.

The test on the City of San Francisco had been performed using the non-pathogenic biological warfare agent simulant called *Bacillus globegii*. The microorganism caused no ill effects in humans or animals but its spores approximated those of deadly *Bacillus anthrasis,* the causative organism of Anthrax. By daybreak on September 20th, a handful of scientists from Fort Detrick began swarming over the San Francisco area where they were busy collecting hundreds of all-glass impinger air-samplers from the government offices and warehouses where they had been covertly installed before the test. The air samplers had faithfully monitored the dispersion and concentration of the simulated biological weapon aerosol.

Tremendous Potential

When the sampling results were analyzed, the Detrick scientists were shocked to discover that the simulated biological aerosol had traveled more than 10 miles from its release point offshore. Had the disseminated agent actually been anthrax spores instead of harmless *Bacillus globegii,* then virtually the entire area population of San Francisco would have received an infective dose and would have died in a matter of a few days. Biological warfare had now progressed from being a battlefield weapon to a strategic weapon in the same category as the atomic bomb, capable of destroying entire cities. In fear, the United States established the original *Epidemic Intelligence Service* designed to detect and provide early warning of a covert biological attack.

Over the next 25 years, new dry formulations of biological warfare munitions were developed and tested out in the vast expanse of the Dugway Proving Grounds in Utah. Small backpack generators were created to disseminate liquid biological agents for use in military special operations, and open air testing revealed the tremendous devastation that could be caused by even such simple but well-engineered devices. As biological munitions development continued, the vast acreage of Dugway proving grounds proved insufficient, and open air testing moved out to the H-bomb testing sites in the Pacific.

By the 1960's, biological warfare had become a well-understood and terrifying new science. Using advanced aerial-delivered systems, it had been demonstrated on live rhesus monkeys. The latter revealed that a single aircraft disseminating a properly formatted biological aerosol could cause infection and death of up to 30 percent of the inhabitants within a 2,400 square kilometer area. During this time, Russian intelligence had a secret informer at Fort Detrick, and the Soviet Union responded by expanding their own biological weapons program and munitions.

It soon became clear that biological weapons were a genie that must never be let out of the bottle, and in 1969 President Nixon terminated all U.S. biological weapon research and production. This was not the case for other nations. In response to the U.S. "Star Wars" program for ballistic missile defense, the Soviet Union began a massive program of offensive biological warfare, loading horrendous disease agents such as the Marburg virus and Smallpox into nose cones of some intercontinental missiles.

> *If the terrorists of the world did not previously know the potential of biological weapons for their cause before [the successful bioterror anthrax letters in 2001], the U.S. media made sure that now they would.*

The Soviet program remained a complete secret to the Western intelligence agencies until three defectors from the program managed to escape from Russia. That program was eventually confirmed by Boris Yeltsin. Then, as the former Soviet Union disintegrated, over 100 Soviet biological warfare scientists found their way to Iran and other parts of the world. They brought with them their expertise in the design and manufacture of a variety of biological munitions, both simple and highly sophisticated. Some of these countries were known to be sponsors of international terrorism.

Biological Weapons and Terrorism

By the onset of the 21st Century, the concept of asymmetrical warfare and the use of terrorism had come into the foreground as large, well-funded, and state-sponsored terrorist groups sprang up throughout the world. In research published only a decade ago, the U.S. Centers for Disease Control and Prevention had estimated that the cost for managing a biological terrorist attack using anthrax spores would be 26.2 billion dollars per 100,000 actual infected cases.

Following the anthrax letter incidents in 2001 in the United States, a flurry of books, internet articles, and mostly clueless "talking heads" on international television, openly described the necessary characteristics of a successful biological aerosol, and one former FBI agent even went so far as to actually name one of the classified additives used for dry biological agent preparation. If the terrorists of the world did not previously know the potential of biological weapons for their cause before, the U.S. media made sure that now they would.

Although federal efforts involving numerous agencies to combat the threat of bioterrorism expanded rapidly following the 2011 anthrax letter attacks, which killed five people and infected 17 others, various congressional commissions, nongovernmental organizations, industry representatives and other experts have highlighted flaws in these activities. A 2008 report published by the congressionally-mandated Commission on the Prevention of WMD Proliferation and Terrorism concluded that "... *unless the world community acts decisively and with great urgency, it is more likely than not that a weapon of mass destruction will be used in a terrorist attack in the world by the end of 2013.*" It went on to say "*The Commission further believes that terrorists are more likely to be able to obtain and use a biological weapon than a nuclear weapon.*"

Making matters worse, unlike most other terrorist attacks, a biological attack could infect victims without their knowledge, and days could pass before victims develop deadly symptoms. To address this problem, the U.S. has been forced to implement air quality monitors throughout the country and stockpile antibiotics for emergency use.

A 2011 study conducted by the Congressional Research Service observes that: *"Unfortunately, the nature of the bioterrorism threat, with its high consequences and low frequency, makes determining the bioterrorism risk difficult. Additionally, the presence of an intelligent adversary who can adapt to the presence of successful countermeasures complicates the use of standard assessment techniques."*

We should never doubt that terrorist adversaries are intelligent, have sophisticated and ever-advancing capabilities to inflict devastating casualties, or fully lack the will to do so. To believe otherwise could potentially be a deadly mistake.

3

Billions to Stem an Unlikely Bioterror Attack

Merrill Goozner

Merrill Goozner is the author of The $800 Million Pill: The Truth Behind the Cost of New Drugs, *a former foreign correspondent, and a contributing reporter to several publications in the areas of economics and investigative business.*

Billions of dollars are spent by the US government to prepare in the event that there is a biological attack. Despite the fact that a terrorist attack on US soil with biological agents is an extremely unlikely scenario, the funds under the Pandemic and All-Hazards Preparedness Act are likely to be reauthorized. Some scientists welcome the influx of money and say that the funding benefits other areas of medicine, such as developing new broad-spectrum antibiotics and antiviral medications. Others complain, however, that the focus on antibioterrorism efforts has distracted from more important medical research.

Republicans and Democrats agreeing on industrial policy to save the auto industry? Unthinkable.

Republicans and Democrats agreeing on industrial policy to promote clean energy companies? Absurd.

But Republicans and Democrats agreeing on industrial policy for the pharmaceutical industry to develop drugs and vaccines to combat bioterror agents? It not only passed by unanimous consent in the Senate earlier this month [March

2012], it will likely be approved by the conference committee that will soon consider the $4.5 billion Pandemic and All-Hazards Preparedness Act (PAHPA), the reauthorization of the 2006 law coordinating the nation's decade-long effort to prepare for a terrorist biological warfare attack [passed January 3, 2013].

A High Price Tag

Despite the reality that the only bioterrorist attack that has ever taken place on U.S. soil (one week after 9/11 [2001]) was launched by a rogue U.S. scientist who had worked in the Cold War biological weapons program and was one of the world's few experts in weaponizing anthrax [in 2001, letters intentionally laced with the spores of the anthrax disease, which is caused by the bacterium Bacillus anthracis, were mailed to victims], the nation has spent an estimated $66 billion in the past decade preparing for the next assault. Tens of billions of dollars have been poured into basic science and applied research to develop vaccines and drugs to combat diseases like anthrax, smallpox (a disease that no longer occurs naturally on earth), botulism and plague.

> *The goal of this basic research is to lay the groundwork for developing broad-spectrum antibiotics and antivirals . . . and multi-platform technologies that potentially could be used to more efficiently develop vaccines against a variety of infectious agents.*

Billions more has gone into beefing up the public health system's ability to respond to emergency health crises. Hospitals have been paid to expand their capacity to respond to surges of patients stricken by a pandemic or a terrorist attack. These nationwide grant programs have helped build a broad base of political support for the programs.

And now, in the reauthorization bill sponsored by Sen. Richard Burr, R-N.C., Congress has earmarked $50 million for a "strategic investor" venture capital fund to invest in start-up biotechnology companies that are developing drugs and vaccines that combat bioterror pathogens. Structured as a public-private partnership outside the government, the goal is to bring more private funding into the hunt for new "counter-measure" products. It will be added to the $450 million a year the government already doles out in grants to companies through the Biomedical Advanced Research and Development Authority (BARDA) and the $2.9 billion earmarked over the next five years for procurement of new drugs and vaccines for government stockpiles.

As the votes in Congress attest (the House version of the bill also passed on a voice vote), the massive commitment to biodefense spending in the 2000s has won broad support from the nation's research and scientific establishment. The National Institute for Allergies and Infectious Diseases (NIAID), headed since the 1980s by Anthony Fauci, receives over $1 billion a year for bioterror-oriented scientific research. The National Cancer Institute, by comparison, receives about $5 billion to look for cures for the tumors that kill over a half million Americans annually.

Officials at NIAID and legislators on Capitol Hill say the massive investment in preventing and curing diseases that rarely if ever occur naturally is providing a huge boost to the moribund U.S. effort to develop new antibiotics to fight the drug resistant bacterial strains that are causing tens of thousands of deaths annually in U.S. hospitals. "The goal of this basic research is to lay the groundwork for developing broad-spectrum antibiotics and antivirals—drugs that can prevent or treat diseases caused by multiple types of bacteria or viruses—and multi-platform technologies that potentially could be used to more efficiently develop vaccines against a variety of infectious agents," the agency says on its website.

But some scientists complain that the anti-bioterror research agenda has detracted from research that specifically targets infectious diseases that are already killing people, both in the U.S. and in the developing world. "I'm sure other programs are reduced because of the money we've put into this," said Peter Agre, director of the Johns Hopkins Malaria Research Institute and winner of the 2003 Nobel Prize in chemistry for his work on cell membrane channels. "We're seeing scientists who have to prematurely end their careers because they can't get grants. Is this bioterror the most important and cost-effective research being done on infectious diseases? I don't think it is."

However, the leaders of the Infectious Diseases Society of America, which represents the medical specialists and researchers in the field, back the program because it creates a stream of funding that otherwise wouldn't exist. "While we understand the nation's current fiscal pressures, we believe that greater investment in key areas is crucial to protect the American people and others from biothreats, pandemics and emerging infections," Thomas Slama, the group's president, wrote in a letter to House and Senate leaders last month [February 2012].

Beefed up biodefense spending also gets championed by the movement to broaden the pipeline of new antibiotics being developed by the pharmaceutical industry. Their argument is the same as NIAID's: a new drug that fights an anthrax infection could also be used to treat the drug-resistant hospital-acquired infections that kill tens of thousands of Americans a year.

"BARDA has pumped $200 million into critical developmental molecules that would either be dead or much less further along if BARDA wasn't around," said Brad Spellberg, a professor of medicine at the Los Angeles Biomedical Research Institute. He also consults for numerous drug companies working on new antibiotics. "The government has become a resource for companies that are not well capitalized."

4

Bioterrorism Funding Withers as Death Germs Thrive in Labs, Nature

Lynne Peeples

Lynne Peeples is an environment and public health reporter.

New and lethal superbugs are continually being developed in nature, making it easy for the average person to get their hands on a potentially deadly agent. Since there is little difference between a pandemic that spreads naturally and one spread by terrorists, funding devoted to fighting these bacteria can benefit both of these causes. Despite this fact, federal funding to fight biological threats is continually cut. The reduced funding makes it more difficult to keep laboratory facilities safe. Funding should therefore be increased for biological research to help prepare us for a natural or terrorist-induced pandemic.

In early October 2001, just days after Bob Stevens hiked through North Carolina's Chimney Rock Park and drank from a waterfall, government officials were retracing his steps. They were desperate to know why the 63-year-old man lay gravely ill in a Florida hospital. His diagnosis: anthrax [disease caused by the bacterium Bacillus anthracis].

"We scratched our heads," says Dr. D.A. Henderson, who served as the first director of the U.S. Office of Public Health

Emergency Preparedness following Sept. 11 [2001]. While anthrax can thrive in nature, and has been known to kill livestock, human exposure is very rare. Nevertheless, officials searched for evidence of this bacterial disease, covering a trail between Stevens' herb garden in Lantana, Fla., and an Irish Pub in Charlotte, N.C. Nothing surfaced. It wasn't until several days later, when more anthrax cases popped up in New York City, that it became clear that this was an unnatural and deliberate attack—delivered via a tainted letter.

Stevens' death marked the country's first known casualty of bioterrorism. Yet the attack was hardly the first use of a living weapon.

Biological weapons have a long and sordid history, from catapulting infected corpses to dropping bombs of plague-infected fleas. But what if a biological weapon were being developed and studied by scientists that had the potential to kill not a battalion or a city, but 150 million people? According to some public health and defense officials, that is exactly what we're facing, following the cultivation of a highly contagious form of H5N1—a lethal bug better known as bird flu. The contagion, they fear, could escape the lab or its recipe could land in the wrong hands.

This work being done in labs in Wisconsin and the Netherlands could also be carried out by nature itself, experts point out. And a super flu is just one of a growing list of potential pandemics that could develop in the near future, either as a result of terrorism, of superbugs leaping from animals to humans, or both.

This was a case where we could really kill two birds with one stone.

In fact, nearly 80 percent of the bioterrorism agents recognized by the U.S. government started in animals. "Many of them were considered for use as such agents only after they emerged from nature as a result of transmission from animals to humans," says Dr. Thomas Monath, who formerly headed a CIA [Central Intelligence Agency] advisory group on ways to counter biological attack. "And nature will spawn new agents continuously."

This means a terrorist may need few tools, little training, minimal money and no published blueprint to harvest a superbug and then unleash it in food, water, air or via insect vectors such as fleas or mosquitos. "As a normal person, you can collect anthrax in Texas soil or ebola in Africa by hunting down a monkey," says Ramon Flick, chief scientific officer at BioProtection Systems Corp., which develops anti-viral vaccines. "It's so easy to get a potential bioterror agent in your hands."

The overlap of bioterrorism agents and emerging infectious disease also means that officials could defend against biological attacks and natural outbreaks in tandem. Laura Kahn, a research scholar at the Woodrow Wilson School of Public and International Affairs at Princeton University, recalls being "dumbstruck" when she made the realization.

"It seemed like this was a case where we could really kill two birds with one stone," she says.

However, no sooner had the realization been made than federal funding cuts began to threaten U.S. efforts to predict and control potentially lethal outbreaks.

Clear and Present Danger

At the United Nations last September [2011], President Barack Obama spoke of the need to "come together to prevent and detect and fight every kind of biological danger, whether it's a pandemic like H1N1, or a terrorist threat, or a terrible disease."

In December [2011], at the Seventh Review Conference of the Biological Weapons Convention, Secretary of State Hillary Rodham Clinton got more specific. Al-Qaida [terrorist organization responsible for September 11, 2001, attacks], she said, was known to be seeking "brothers with degrees in microbiology or chemistry to develop weapons of mass destruction."

"There are warning signs," added Clinton, "and they are too serious to ignore."

Yet federal funding to prevent and respond to bioterrorism is plummeting. The U.S. Centers for Disease Control and Prevention's [CDC] biodefense budget peaked in 2005 at about $1.2 billion. The 2012 budget is down to $800 million, with state and local programs—the country's first line of defense—absorbing some of the most significant cuts.

"We haven't had enough resources to do as much training. It's taking longer to revise plans so they may not be as current," says Jane Braun, director of the Office of Emergency Preparedness at the Minnesota Department of Health. "It's hurting our ability to respond as rapidly and as effectively. And this is true for all states."

The [Weapons of Mass Destruction Terrorism Research Center's] "report card" concluded that the U.S. "remains largely unprepared for a large-scale bioterrorism attack or deadly disease outbreak."

Over the last decade, Minnesota has provided outreach to local labs, including hands-on training for germs that are rarely seen. Every year, the state highlights four or five new organisms.

The effort has paid off. Last August [2011], an individual traveling through Minnesota landed in a rural hospital that had participated in the training. Workers quickly recognized the culprit as anthrax—in this case, naturally acquired—and "saved the guy's life," says Maureen Sullivan, also of the Minnesota Department of Public Health and chair of the Public Health Preparedness and Response Committee for the Association of Public Health Laboratories.

Sullivan is now working with less than half of the lab funding she received from the CDC in 2003. The cuts mean less hands-on training, fewer organisms, and inconsistent coordination between state and local labs. "The general public, and I could go as far as saying politicians or the people with the money, don't really realize the importance of sustaining the infrastructure we've created," Sullivan says.

Further, the Biomedical Advanced Research and Development Authority receives about 10 percent of the funding it needs to develop antibiotics and other medical defenses, according to the bipartisan Weapons of Mass Destruction Terrorism Research Center. "A bio-response enterprise without adequate medical countermeasures is like an Army without bullets—it may look good on a parade ground, but has minimal value for national security," says an October [2011] publication from the center. The center's "report card" concluded that the U.S. "remains largely unprepared for a large-scale bioterrorism attack or deadly disease outbreak."

None of this is to say the the U.S. hasn't improved bioterrorism preparedness since the 2001 anthrax attacks. The subsequent surge in funds has gone a long way.

"We've made a lot of progress," says Dr. Ali Khan, director of the CDC Office of Public Health Preparedness and Response. "But that progress is in jeopardy."

Fuzzy Lines

Some of the progress also turns out to be a double-edged sword. The rise of biotechnology is a case in point.

In January [2012], the Dutch and American researchers behind the two widely-discussed H5N1 papers, along with dozens of other flu experts, voluntarily halted bird flu research to give the world time to digest and discuss the dangers.

As its name suggests, the virus mainly affects birds. Sick birds have infected human handlers on rare occasions, but the inability of the virus to jump directly between humans has kept outbreaks from becoming pandemics. In the two not-yet-published studies, scientists tweaked the virus so it could spread easily among ferrets, a popular stand-in for people in flu research.

In an editorial published in late-January in the journal *Science*, Ron Fouchier and his Dutch co-authors argue that their bird flu research and its publication are crucial for understanding what traits to look for if (or more likely, when) the virus mutates into a more contagious, deadly or drug-resistant bug—with or without human help. Such knowledge could help contain dangerous viruses in the future. The public health benefits, they wrote, far outweigh the risks.

New regulations are in the works to require labs using certain biological agents to implement safeguards including psychological evaluations for employees.

The scientists are also far from alone in their tinkering. "To a certain extent, the genie is out of the bottle," says Dr. Scott Lillibridge of Texas A&M [Health Science Center], formerly the founding director of the Bioterrorism Preparedness and Response Program at the CDC. "We have moved from dozens of labs when we started biodefense in the U.S. to probably thousands of labs [worldwide] that dabble in genetic manipulation."

Greg Koblentz, a biosecurity expert at George Mason University in Virginia, adds that labs around the world are inconsistent in their safety and security standards. Nevertheless, he says that "we still shouldn't be going around making new versions" of deadly viruses without fully considering the possible implications.

Even in the U.S., decreasing funds are making it more difficult to maintain safe and secure facilities, says Minnesota's Sullivan. New regulations are in the works to require labs using certain biological agents to implement safeguards including psychological evaluations for employees. But the added cost has led many states to consider dropping out of the program altogether, Sullivan says.

Meanwhile, nature knows no rules or regulations and continues to create new viruses and alter old ones. And because animal-borne diseases may need no help spilling over into humans, outbreak investigations could easily confuse intentional and natural outbreaks.

A 1999 *New Yorker* article quoted an advisor to the FBI [Federal Bureau of Investigation] who was looking into the possibility that West Nile had been deliberately introduced into New York—a hypothesis later dismissed: "If I was planning a bioterror event, I'd do things with subtle finesse, to make it look like a natural outbreak," the advisor said. "That would delay the response and lock up the decision-making process."

"Insidious" Ignorance

It took the CDC and the FBI several days to confirm the 2001 anthrax attacks and to inform the public. At that point, "it was a madhouse," says Henderson, now a distinguished scholar at the Center for Biosecurity of the University of Pittsburgh Medical Center.

He recalls everything from talcum powder to women's facial powder arriving at labs for testing. "The worst," says Henderson, "were the powdered donuts."

In all, 22 people got sick and five died. Things could have been much worse. The same quantity of dry-powdered anthrax released into the ventilation system of the World Trade Center could have killed far more people than the airplane attacks did on 9/11 [2001], according to a 2006 statement from Dr. Margaret Hamburg, the current FDA [US Food and Drug Administration] Administrator.

When Henderson took charge of the new public health preparedness operation following the World Trade Center attacks, he learned that intelligence warned of a possible second event, this one biologic. Henderson says that he had already been trying to persuade people that the country should be concerned about biological agents, but was confronted with little interest. "People thought it was morally repugnant to even think about it," he says.

Anyone that turns a blind eye to these [biological] threats perplexes me.

That ignorance remained widespread; Henderson witnessed the consequences. As people evacuated from buildings in response to the anthrax attacks, he explains, many were taken into back lots to be hosed down: "That does no good. Not for a biologic agent."

Despite the chaos, the nation quickly returned to complacency.

The potential for another attack of anthrax or other lethal living agent remains high today. Henderson warns that it is "entirely possible and likely" that a "relative amateur" could pluck strains from the environment that would be just as virulent as the anthrax used in the mailings.

Elin Gursky, a health preparedness policy expert at the public-service research institute ANSER/Analytic Services Inc., also highlights Iran's biological weapon program and the host of emerging pathogens. "Anyone that turns a blind eye to these threats perplexes me," she says.

Gursky calls the current "erosion" of funding "insidious."

"Biological Chernobyl"

When an estimated 100 people died of anthrax near Sverdlovsk (now Ekaterinberg, Russia) in 1979, the Soviet government blamed the environment. Anthrax was endemic to the area, so it was plausible that the local meat became contaminated by livestock grazing in a pasture naturally laden with the spores.

Years later, however, American scientists called the Soviets out on their deliberate misrepresentation—and their violation of the 1972 Biological Weapons Convention, a treaty that bans these weapons.

By mapping both human and animal cases, and the direction of the wind, U.S. scientists established the path of the airborne agent and concluded that the so-called "biological Chernobyl" had actually originated from a secret military facility, says Dr. Peter Rabinowitz, an environmental medicine expert at the Yale University School of Medicine.

The accidental release of anthrax killed animals over a far wider range than it killed people who breathed the spores. This is not surprising, given that livestock spend more time outside and have greater susceptibility to anthrax than humans. But the implications could be powerful. If local farmers and veterinarians had recognized the animal infections and shared their findings with medical doctors, early courses of antibiotics may have saved human lives.

"The government spends a lot of money developing biosensors," says Princeton's Kahn, referring to air sampling surveillance and other sophisticated systems. "But I would argue the best ones are flying around," or in this case, hanging out on farms.

Zoos can be particularly good sources of sentinels, she adds, as they house a wide array of animals from around the world with different levels of susceptibility. Most zoos are also located near densely populated urban centers, which tend to be terrorism "hot spots."

"There's a possibility that the high-tech tools are not even in the right place," says Rabinowitz. "By being constantly aware of new events in animals as well as in humans and the environment, we're more likely to pick up a new threat."

The strategy could address the risk of a less direct terrorist attack, such as the exploitation of a vulnerable water or food system. Plants and animals have little or no innate resistance to foreign pathogens, and are not vaccinated against the bugs. Regardless of whether the agent spills over into humans, losses could easily run into the billions of dollars.

"The means of efficient dissemination by a terrorist would not involve complex delivery systems—just a needle and a cow in a pasture," says Monath, now an adjunct professor at the Harvard School of Public Health.

Because the [Rift Valley fever] disease is not considered a priority human bioterrorism agent by the government, research funding is low.

Koblentz, of George Mason, says he doesn't see such "subtle" attacks lining up with a terrorist's M.O., or the "idea of getting attention towards a cause and coercing the government to change its behavior." But he does agree with the need for broad surveillance. "If we only start paying attention when people are dying, at that point it's too late," says Koblentz.

Are We "Ready for Anything"?

This emphasis on coordination among medical, veterinary and environmental health scientists, reflecting the global "One Health" movement, could also be employed in the development of vaccines and treatments for bioterror threats.

Rift Valley fever virus is a prime candidate for such collaboration, says BioProtection Systems' Flick, an expert on emerging infectious disease, which can afflict both animals and humans. Creating a livestock vaccine would reduce the risk of human infection. However, because the disease is not considered a priority human bioterrorism agent by the government, research funding is low. Jason McDonald, a CDC spokesperson, explains the agency's exclusion of Rift Valley:

humans typically contract the virus through bites of infected mosquitoes and just 1 percent of these victims die.

Flick disagrees.

The public's current awareness of Rift Valley fever and its perception of the West Nile virus threat before 1999 are strikingly similar, he says. West Nile had not been given much thought before it cropped up in New York City. Within a few years it had spread across the country.

Flick warns of even more devastating consequences with the relatively unknown bug. More mosquito species can carry Rift Valley than West Nile. It is also more virulent. And according to research in Arabia and Africa, the fatality rate may actually be increasing, killing more than 30 percent of people infected during recent outbreaks. Further, there does appear to be potential for human-to-human transmission.

Shortly after the anthrax attacks, experts convened to draft a federal priority list of bioterror agents based on what they perceived as the country's greatest vulnerabilities. Among the top-ranking bugs: anthrax, smallpox and plague.

"We had no ability to know what terrorists would really do," says Scott Lillibridge, who chaired the committee and is now at the Texas A&M Health Science Center. The list was supposed to be temporary, he says, merely helping states and local groups best allocate their first rounds of biodefense funding.

"I don't think it's current," Lillibridge says. He suggests the need to move beyond targeting specific agents towards a broader look at all pathogens, adding that "you've got to be ready for anything."

The CDC's Khan agrees. "If your mind is set on anthrax or smallpox, and you think that we have more than enough vaccine to protect every American, then you might say, 'OK, we're done. Let's close up shop and move on,'" he says. "But we'll never be done with the list of these new agents that show up every day."

Researchers have discovered an average of 15 to 20 previously unknown diseases in each of the past few decades, including incurable diseases like HIV/AIDS, ebola and SARS, with new pathogens likely to emerge and spread faster due to the global population's increasing size and mobility.

Global Health Security

Lillibridge recalls his time in China during the SARS epidemic of 2003. "I was back home [in the U.S.] within 19 hours from Beijing," he says. "I easily could have been incubating something."

At the time, scientists had not yet identified the newly emerging pathogen, which meant no diagnostic tests.

The ability to detect and identify diseases as they initially emerge can go a long way in thwarting an outbreak, he says. It can provide the time to prepare, including upgrading quarantines at the border, researching a vaccine and identifying what drugs might successfully combat the infection.

"A couple weeks can be critical," says Lillibridge. "It can make an administration look foolish or like they're in control."

Overall, the U.S. government spent approximately $60 billion on biodefense from 2001 to 2009. Only 2 percent of that was dedicated to preventive measures such as programs to discover and reduce biological threats overseas, according to Koblentz.

"To protect Americans, we must look at what is going on in the rest of the world," says Khan.

ANSER's Gursky, recently returned from hosting a NATO [North Atlantic Treaty Organization] meeting in Central Europe. "The most important strategy is to build up the capabilities that we share, which means reaching across borders and politics," she says.

Meanwhile, the domestic coordination that President Obama spoke of in September [2011] is still lacking, some experts say. As with terrorism before 9/11, there is no single agency coordinating biosecurity efforts. Lillibridge suggests it's about time for a focused biodefense center, "a functioning unit where you have lab, surveillance and all these programs aligned."

Coalescing efforts might also allow the government to do more with less. "We're looking at not only man being a terrorist, but nature can be a terrorist as well," says Henderson. "The natural occurrence of a disease gives us similar problems, so whatever we're doing to prepare for one, prepares us for the other."

5

The US Food Supply Is Vulnerable to Bioterrorism

Dean Olson

Dean Olson works for the Federal Bureau of Investigation (FBI), where he researches and writes about issues of homeland security.

As evidenced in al Qaeda terrorist training manuals, the American food system's economic importance makes it an attractive target for terrorists. In addition to outside groups, domestic terrorists, economic opportunists, and militant animal rights or environmental activists are all possible agents that would seek to harm the country's food system. Diseases that affect cattle are dangerous because of how quickly they can spread among crowded animal populations. Fruits and vegetables are also uniquely susceptible because they do not require the same processing and cooking procedures that would otherwise kill pathogens. The US food system must be safeguarded.

The United States enjoys a safe, plentiful, and inexpensive food supply. Americans spend only 11 percent of their income on food compared with the global average of 20 to 30 percent. The nation's agricultural abundance helps drive its economic prosperity. As many as 1 of 6 jobs are linked to agriculture, a trillion-dollar industry. Agriculture-related products comprise nearly 10 percent of all U.S. exports, amounting to nearly $68 billion in 2006.

Dean Olson, "Agroterrorism: Threats to America's Economy and Food Supply," *FBI Law Enforcement Bulletin*, February 2012. Reproduced by permission.

Terrorists consider America's agriculture and food production tempting targets. They have noticed that its food supply is among the most vulnerable and least protected of all potential targets of attack. When American and allied forces overran al Qaeda [terrorist organization reponsible for the September 11, 2001, attacks] sanctuaries in the caves of eastern Afghanistan in 2002, among the thousands of documents they discovered were U.S. agricultural documents and al Qaeda training manuals targeting agriculture.

A subset of bioterrorism, *agroterrorism* is defined as "the deliberate introduction of an animal or plant disease for the purpose of generating fear, causing economic losses, or undermining social stability." It represents a tactic to attack the economic stability of the United States. Killing livestock and plants or contaminating food can help terrorists cause economic crises in the agriculture and food industries. Secondary goals include social unrest and loss of confidence in government.

Militant animal rights or environmental activists pose a threat because they consider immoral the use of animals for food.

Agroterrorism Is a Serious Concern

Agroterrorism is not new. The Assyrians poisoned enemy wells with rye ergot during the 6th century B.C. During World War I, German agents in the United States infected horses and cattle in transit across the Atlantic to France. In 1994, in The Dalles, Oregon, a religious cult intentionally contaminated 10 restaurant salad bars with salmonella, sickening more than 750 people in an attempt to influence the outcome of a local election. Since 1912, 12 documented cases have involved the substate use of pathogenic agents to infect livestock or contaminate food.

The agroterrorism threat emanates from four categories of perpetrators. The foremost threat is posed by transnational groups, like al Qaeda—widely believed to present the most probable threat of inflicting economic harm on the United States.

The second group is comprised of economic opportunists tempted to manipulate markets. They understand that a foot and mouth disease (FMD) outbreak, for example, would have a dramatic impact on markets. By introducing the virus, they could exploit the markets for personal economic gain.

The third category includes domestic terrorists who may view the introduction of FMD as a blow against the federal government. As an outlier of this category, the unbalanced individual or disgruntled employee may perpetrate an attack for a variety of idiosyncratic or narcissistic motivations.

Finally, militant animal rights or environmental activists pose a threat because they consider immoral the use of animals for food. Groups, such as the Animal Liberation Front and its sister organization, the Earth Liberation Front, could view an attack on the animal food industry a positive event.

Agroterrorism Increasingly Attractive

Because it lacks the drama and spectacle of more common terrorist violence, such as bombings and murders, agroterrorism has remained a secondary consideration, and no documented attacks in the homeland have occurred since 9/11 [2001]. Several recent factors may have made agroterrorism a more attractive tactic.

First, the threat environment has changed dramatically. America has had recent successes against al Qaeda's leadership. These victories have forced the group to morph in both structure and tactics. The increasingly dangerous environment it now must operate in has prevented it from mounting catastrophic terrorist attacks on the scale of 9/11. Now, al Qaeda places its emphasis on smaller, independent attacks following a "death by a thousand cuts" strategy to exhaust, overwhelm, and distract U.S. Department of Homeland Security forces. The group seeks to flood America's already information overloaded intelligence systems with myriad threats and "background noise." Agroterrorism also may serve as a way to magnify the social upheaval caused by smaller, independent attacks, like bombings.

Second, Osama Bin Ladin [terrorist leader] consistently had argued that attacking the U.S. economy represented the best way to destroy America's ability to project military power abroad. Underpinning this view is al Qaeda's historical narrative that jihad [holy war] against the Soviets following the invasion of Afghanistan led not only to the defeat of the Red Army but, ultimately, to the demise of the U.S.S.R [Union of Soviet Socialist Republics]. As divorced from reality as this view seems, economic harm remains one of the pillars of al Qaeda's terror strategy against the United States. In a video broadcast before the 2004 U.S. presidential elections, Osama Bin Ladin bragged that his organization ". . . bled Russia for 10 years until it went bankrupt and was forced to withdraw in defeat. . . . We are continuing in the same policy to make America bleed profusely to the point of bankruptcy. . . ." He boasted that the 9/11 attacks had cost al Qaeda $500,000 while inflicting a staggering $500 billion in economic losses to America. According to Bin Ladin, "every dollar of al Qaeda defeated a million dollars [of America] . . . besides the loss of a huge number of jobs."

Analysts believe that al Qaeda's evolving tactics increasingly will "focus on targets that will yield the most economic damage." Terrorist leaders realize that America's strength stems largely from its economic vitality. They pursue an overarching strategy that all attacks should focus on weakening America's economic strength, especially through protracted guerilla warfare. In their view, as the United States loses its standing in the Middle East, groups, like al Qaeda, can gain ground and remove from power regimes they view as corrupt and illegitimate.

Terrorists know that a successful agroterrorism incident threatens America's economic welfare and its standing as a leading exporter of agricultural products to the world. A significant disruption in agricultural exports caused by such an attack would have ripple effects in the United States' and global economies. This economic disruption would occur on three levels.

The first involves direct losses due to containment measures, such as stop-movement orders (SMOs) or quarantines of suspected stock. Additional costs would arise from the culling and destruction of disease-ridden livestock. Second, indirect multiplier effects, such as compensation to farmers for destruction of agricultural commodities and losses suffered by directly and indirectly related industries, would arise. And, third, international costs would result from protective trade embargoes. Less measurable consequences would include the undermining of confidence in and support of government, creation of social panic, and threat to public health on the national and global levels.

In an FMD [foot and mouth disease] attack, the animals themselves serve as the primary medium for pathogenic transmission.

Given its ease of execution and low cost to high benefit ratio, agroterrorism fits the evolving strategy of al Qaeda that focuses on inexpensive but highly disruptive attacks in lieu of monumental ones. Agroterrorism could exacerbate the social upheaval caused by random bombings. The ability to employ cheap and unsophisticated means to undermine America's economic base, combined with the added payoff to potentially overwhelm its counterterrorism resources, makes livestock- and food-related attacks increasingly attractive.

Foot and Mouth Disease

Attacks directed against the cattle, swine, or poultry industries or via the food chain pose the most serious danger for latent, ongoing effects and general socioeconomic and political disruption. Experts agree that FMD presents the most ominous threat. Eradicated in the United States in 1929, FMD remains endemic in South America, Africa, and Asia. An especially contagious virus 20 times more infectious than smallpox, FMD causes painful blisters on the tongues, hooves, and teats of cloven-hoofed animals, including cattle, hogs, sheep, goats, and deer, rendering them unable to walk, give milk, eat, or drink. Although people generally cannot contract the disease, they can carry the virus in their lungs for up to 48 hours and transmit it to animals. The animal-to-animal airborne transmission range is 50 miles. An infected animal can shred the virus in large quantities from its upper respiratory tract via drooling, coughing, and discharging mucus. Extremely stable, FMD can survive in straw or clothing for 1 month and spread up to 100 kilometers via the wind. Because herds exist as highly crowded populations bred and reared in extremely close proximity to one another, a significant risk exists that such pathogenic agents as FMD will spread well beyond the locus of a specific outbreak before health officials become aware of a problem. An FMD outbreak could spread to as many as 25 states in as little as 5 days simply through the regulated movement of animals from farm to market.

From a tactical perspective, an FMD attack holds appeal for several reasons. First, unlike biological warfare directed against humans, no issue of weaponization exists. In an FMD attack, the animals themselves serve as the primary medium for pathogenic transmission, and countries as close as those in South America offer a ready source of the virus. As one analyst described it, the virus "can be spread by simply wiping the mucus from an infected animal on a handkerchief and then transferring the virus to healthy animals by wiping their noses . . . by stopping on a highway in rural America and releasing the virus among curious livestock an outbreak could be initiated."

Second, FMD is nonzoonotic, presenting no risk of accidental human infection. There exists no need for elaborate personal protective equipment or an advanced understanding of animal disease science. In a biowarfare attack targeting people, the deadly pathogen poses a threat to the perpetrators, as well as their intended victims. Preparing the pathogen so that terrorists can handle it safely yet disseminate it effectively to intended victims can prove difficult. For instance, the Aum Shinrikyo [Japanese cult] sarin gas attacks on the Tokyo subway in 1994 largely failed to kill the number of people intended due to the crude method of dissemination.

Third, terrorists could introduce and subsequently disperse the virus throughout the American food production system through multiple carriers, including animals carrying and introducing it into susceptible herds; animals exposed to contraband materials, such as contaminated food, hay, feedstuffs, hides, or biologics; people wearing clothing or using equipment, including tractors and trucks, to transmit the virus to uninfected animals; and contaminated facilities, such as feed yards, sale barns, and trucks that commonly hold or transport susceptible animals.

The same factors that yield inexpensive and plentiful food by promoting maximum production efficiency also make American agricultural systems inherently vulnerable. The highly concentrated and intensive nature of livestock production encourages the rapid spread of contagious pathogens. Most dairies house at least 1,500 cows, with the largest facilities containing 10,000. Animals often are born on breeding farms and then transported to another state for slaughtering and processing. Otherwise isolated and widely dispersed farms often share equipment, vehicles, and veterinary instruments. Feedlots and auctions routinely intermingle animals from a wide geographic area. On average, a pound of meat travels 1,000 miles before it reaches the consumer's table.

The introduction of FMD would require the mass slaughter and disposal of infected animals. An outbreak could halt the domestic and international sale of meat and meat products for years. In this regard, in 2001, FMD in the United Kingdom affected 9,000 farms and required the destruction of more than 4,000,000 animals. Researchers believe that a similar outbreak in the United States would cost taxpayers up to $60 billion. An FMD attack could result in massive herd culling, the need to destroy processed goods, and extensive decontamination efforts of production and livestock-containment facilities. Most Americans have not witnessed the intense media coverage of high-volume culling operations involving the destruction and disposal of tens of thousands of animals. Large-scale eradication and disposal of livestock likely would be especially controversial as it affects farmers and ranchers and offends the sensibilities of animal rights activists and environmental organizations.

> The laws of many states treat agroterrorism as a crime investigation, giving local law enforcement agencies primary responsibility.

Food Production and Distribution

If terrorists strive for human deaths, the food production and distribution chain offers a low-tech but effective mechanism for disseminating toxins and bacteria, such as botulism, E. coli, and salmonella. Developments in the farm-to-table continuum greatly have increased the number of entry points for these agents. Many food processing and packing plants employ large, unscreened seasonal workforces. They commonly operate uneven standards of internal quality and inadequate biosurveillance control to detect adulteration. These vulnerabilities, combined with the lack of security at many processing and packing plants, contribute to the ease of perpetrating a food-borne attack.

Beyond the economic and political impact, low-tech bioterrorist assaults against the food chain have the potential to create social panic as people lose confidence in the safety of the food supply. A large-scale attack potentially could undermine the public's confidence in its government. Because most processed food travels to distribution centers within a matter of hours, a single case of chemical or biological adulteration could have significant latent ongoing effects, particularly if the source of the contamination is not immediately apparent and there are acute ailments or deaths. Supermarkets in major American cities stock only a 7-day supply of food; therefore, any significant and continuing disruption in supply quickly will lead to severe shortages.

Experts believe that fruit- and vegetable-packing plants are among the most vulnerable venues for food-borne attacks. Many represent small-scale manufacturers that specialize in ready-to-eat meats or aggregated foodstuffs. They do not practice uniform biosecurity methods, and they do not use heat, an effective front-end barrier against pathogens, in food processing. Also, because they deal in already-prepared produce that does not require cooking—a good back-end defense against microbial introduction—they provide a viable portal to introduce pathogens.

Law Enforcement Preparedness

Farms, ranches, and feedlots in America are dispersed, open, and generally unprotected. The majority of state and local law enforcement agencies face financial and strategic challenges when responding to agroterrorism, yet the laws of many states treat agroterrorism as a crime investigation, giving local law enforcement agencies primary responsibility.

An outbreak of FMD would exhaust law enforcement resources quickly. After recognition of the disease by state agriculture authorities, subsequent steps in the emergency response involve containment and eradication, often involving multiple herds and a large quarantine area that may encompass multiple counties. State agriculture authorities working with the U.S. Department of Agriculture's Animal and Plant Health Inspection Service have responsibility and authority for animal disease. Specially trained animal health officials make decisions on disease control, such as livestock quarantine and the timing and method of livestock depopulation—culling, destroying, and disposing of diseased animals from infected herds by burning or burial.

Following strict biosecurity measures can prevent the spread of disease. Local and state law enforcement would play a pivotal role in this effort by adhering to three primary responsibilities.

First, police officials would enforce quarantine orders given by state agriculture authorities. This involves isolating and containing infected stock to prevent the spread of disease. A quarantine area would comprise a 6-mile radius, approximately 113 square miles, surrounding the point of origin; numerous roadblocks would prevent vehicles, equipment, or persons from entering or leaving without detailed decontamination measures and authorization. Inside the quarantine area, officials would establish an "exposed zone" in which all cloven-hoofed animals would be destroyed. For effectiveness, quarantine of infected premises and SMOs would have to remain in effect for a minimum of 30 days.

The second responsibility occurs in conjunction with quarantine. Officers would enforce SMOs issued by the state governor to prevent the spread of the disease. Initial biosecurity efforts could require placement of all animals under an SMO.

Law enforcement may be empowered to restrict human and animal movement in and out of the quarantine zone. This authority would include all animals in transit within a wide geographic area until the investigation clarified the extent of the infection and determined which animals can move safely. Although FMD affects only cloven-hoofed animals, humans, horses, and other animals may carry the virus.

Enforcing an SMO would require care and shelter for animals in transit that must be temporarily unloaded and housed at local sites providing feed and water. During the SMO, law enforcement would interview drivers to determine points of origin and destinations of animals. Research indicates that officers would stop and evaluate an average of nearly 50 vehicles per hour in the first day of an SMO.

Third, the criminal investigation of the outbreak further would tax already strained law enforcement resources. The investigation would focus on identifying the source of the virus and the mechanism used to infect susceptible animals. The danger of additional infections by the perpetrators would make the criminal investigation time sensitive.

Many law enforcement agencies lack the sufficient resources and procedures to simultaneously cope with quarantines, SMOs, and criminal investigations while also staffing widely dispersed checkpoints around the clock for the duration of the emergency. When combined with the need also to deliver routine law enforcement services, most agencies would struggle to meet these demands, especially during the protracted nature of an FMD outbreak.

Agriculture may not represent terrorists' first choice of targets because it lacks the shock factor of more traditional attacks; however, it comprises the largest single sector in the U.S. economy, making agroterrorism a viable primary aspiration. Such terrorist groups as al Qaeda have made economic and trade disruption key goals. They believe that by imposing economic hardship on America, its citizens will tire of the struggle and force their elected leaders to withdraw from commitments abroad.

6

Are Syria, Iran Playing Obama for a Fool?

Frida Ghitis

Frida Ghitis is a world affairs columnist for The Miami Herald *and* World Politics Review *and a former CNN producer and correspondent.*

Believing that the United States will not enforce Syria's agreement to relinquish its stockpile of chemical weapons, Syria has been slow to comply. As long as the Syrians view the United States as weak, no other diplomatic approaches will be successful. The United States must take a harder stance against Syria to ensure that their chemical weapons are destroyed.

Remember Syria's chemical weapons? Yes, those, the ones the Syrian regime agreed to give up after President [Barack] Obama threatened to bomb.

All of the "priority one," the most dangerous of those weapons, were supposed to be gone by December 31 [2013] last year. They're not. Almost all of them—more than 95%—are still in Syria despite a commitment by the Syrian President Bashar al-Assad to get rid of his deadly arsenal.

The deal to remove Syria's stock of WMD [Weapons of Mass Destruction] was the one tangible accomplishment of the Obama administration's approach to the Middle East's multiple crises. Now that deal looks to be failing, even as red flags also start flying along the path to a deal with Iran.

It's hard to escape the impression that Iran and its close ally, Syria, are toying with the U.S.

Pursuing a Diplomatic Solution

America is earnestly seeking a diplomatic solution. And we should all hope diplomacy succeeds in securing an agreement that stops the carnage in Syria and one that prevents Iran from becoming a greater threat to its neighbors. But there is a reason these efforts are already running into trouble.

Secretary of State John Kerry is valiantly pursuing the suit-and-tie approach to peace, but Kerry is handicapped by the growing perception that Obama will not use military force under any circumstances. The U.S. doesn't need to release bombs to show it is powerful. What it needs to do is remind its adversaries, its enemies, that it has options beyond the well-appointed rooms of hotels along Lake Geneva [Switzerland].

Syria's al-Assad, who has heard Obama's threats on the use of chemical weapons starting in the summer of 2012, . . . is still playing games with America while relentlessly slaughtering and starving his people.

Obama can do this by speaking directly and firmly about those choices. That alone would go a long way in reshaping some points of views, and could produce results. If it doesn't, more concrete steps would be required, from increasing material support for specific anti-al-Assad forces to a tightening of sanctions against Iran and other steps.

Diplomats can help concentrate the mind of their interlocutors when the people on the other side of the table worry about the possible cost of failure.

This is true of Syria's al-Assad, who has heard Obama's threats on the use of chemical weapons starting in the summer of 2012, and is still playing games with America while relentlessly slaughtering and starving his people.

Iran Also Toying with the United States

And it is true about Iran, which just heard Obama during the State of the Union [January 2014] threaten to veto a plan to set the stage now for additional sanctions against Iran if negotiations fail in the next six months. Iranian officials presumably also heard the president state what so many have stopped believing: that he is prepared "to exercise all options to make sure Iran does not build a nuclear weapon."

The more we hear from the Iranians, the less likely it seems that a successful agreement can be reached.

After CNN's Fareed Zakaria talked to Iranian President Hassan Rouhani last week, he concluded there's a "train wreck" on its way in negotiations. The U.S. is moving forward on the assumption that a deal would involve the dismantling of some key nuclear facilities, but Rouhani, the moderate face of the Islamist Republic, made it "categorically, specifically and unequivocally" clear that Iran has no intention of ever rolling back its nuclear program.

On Syria, I had heard rumors that the removal of its most terrifying weapons was not going as scheduled. Then an anonymous source told Reuters [news agency] that the regime has delivered a dismal 4.1% of the 1,300 tons of toxic agents it has reported, "and there is no sign of more," on the way.

Then the U.S. confirmed it.

On Thursday [January 30, 2014], Ambassador Robert Mikulak, who heads the U.S. delegation to the Organization for the Prohibition of Chemical Weapons, told the group that Syria is ignoring the timeline for removal of banned weapons and displaying "a 'bargaining mentality' rather than a security mentality." In addition, he said, there is little progress on Syria's commitment to destroy its chemical weapons production facilities.

If Syria's games over its chemical weapons sound familiar—agreements followed by "misunderstandings" and endless delays—it is because we see much the same already unfolding with Iran.

Iran's President [Rouhani] and foreign minister [Mohammad Javad Zarif] are well versed in their communications strategy with the West. They are charming and fluent, speaking directly to Western publics who would like nothing better than to be done with the threat of a confrontation. And how great it would be to truly resolve the issue diplomatically.

Hope, however, is not a strategy any more than closing your eyes when you don't like what you see, as when Iranian President Hassan Rouhani tweeted that in the Geneva agreement the "world powers surrendered" to Iran. That's when the White House dismissed the worrisome statement as a play for a domestic audience.

Since then, however, one after another Iranian official has maintained they have no intention of taking apart any of their nuclear program. Without destroying any centrifuges, reactors, or other facilities, Iran can negotiate with the West, and receive political, diplomatic and economic benefits from the loosening of sanctions, as it already has. And then, as top Iranian officials have said, it can reverse any freeze and resume high-level enrichment in 24 hours. That's the vow from the top nuclear negotiator and the foreign minister.

Making matters worse, much worse, we have just learned that American intelligence officials believe Iran has essentially already reached the "nuclear breakout" capability it sought. Director of National Intelligence James Clapper told Congress this week that Iran has made "technical progress in a number of areas—including uranium enrichment, nuclear reactors, and ballistic missiles—from which it could draw if it decided to build missile-deliverable nuclear weapons." In other words, he concluded, the only thing between Iran and nuclear weapons is a political decision to build the bomb. Everything else is already in place.

That extraordinary revelation received little attention in the U.S., where the headlines were consumed with the crisis in ice-logged Atlanta [Georgia]. In other places, the news was cause for alarm. "Heaven help us," tweeted a respected Israeli journalist, "Iran can now build and deliver nukes."

How is it possible that Iran and Syria are getting away with this?

Iran and Syria are not the only countries convinced that the U.S. will not take military action. Saudi Arabia apparently has reached much the same conclusion.

After his 2012 red lines became blurred, the deal to get rid of al-Assad's chemical weapons allowed Obama to claim he had succeeded in showing consequences for their use, even if al-Assad stayed in place and the killing continued. But now it looks as if essentially nothing has changed. Except that tens of thousands more have died.

To support American diplomacy, Obama needs to erase that image of a weak America. Again, there is no need to launch attacks and deploy troops. But there is a need to show to America's enemies they cannot play the U.S. for a fool. The President needs to assert convincingly that he will be able to exercise power if that becomes necessary. Nothing would be more helpful to the chances for diplomatic success.

7

US Has No Legal Basis for Action in Syria but That Won't Stop Us

Eric Posner

Eric Posner is the Kirkland and Ellis Professor of Law at the University of Chicago Law School. He is also an editor at The Journal of Legal Studies, *where he has published numerous articles on issues of international law.*

The United States has attempted to offer legal justification for military action in the past, but the efforts have fallen short. War is too complex and unpredictable to be able to prepare guidelines that can be followed in the midst of conflict. While it is true that the United States has acted and will likely continue to act without legal basis, this is necessary. In order to secure the safety of the nation, the president must have the ability to act quickly as threats arise.

*I*nter arma enim silent leges, said the Romans—in times of war, the law falls silent. But ours is a chattier society. Rather than keep silent, our laws speak loudly about war. We just don't follow them—as the U.S. military intervention in Syria is about to show.

Press reports [August 2013] say that President [Barack] Obama has ordered his lawyers to supply him with a legal justification for a military assault on Syria, and unnamed officials have cited the Geneva Protocol, the Chemical Weapons Convention, the Kosovo precedent, and the so-called Responsibility to Protect doctrine. They have not cited the United Nations [U.N.] Charter, which flatly bans military interventions without Security Council approval, which the United States cannot obtain because of Russian and Chinese opposition.

No Authorization for Military Action

The Geneva Protocol of 1925 (which Syria ratified) and the Chemical Weapons Convention of 1993 (which Syria has not ratified) ban the use of chemical weapons, but do not authorize countries to attack other countries that violate these treaties. The United States has no more authority to attack Syria for violating these treaties than it does to bomb Europe for giving import preferences to Caribbean banana producers in violation of international trade law. At one time, countries could use military force as "countermeasures" against treaty violators, but only against violators that harmed the country in question—and Syria has not used chemical weapons against the United States—but in any event, that rule has been superseded by the U.N. Charter.

> *Virtually all major countries have broken the rules from time to time, even the saintly European countries that joined in the Kosovo intervention.*

The Kosovo precedent refers to the 1999 military intervention in Serbia, launched to stop a campaign of ethnic cleansing against people living in that region of Serbia. Then, too, the United States failed to obtain approval from the Security Council but attacked anyway. It's odd to claim the Kosovo attack as a precedent, as it was widely regarded as illegal at the time and afterward.

But most people, or at least Westerners, believed that the Kosovo intervention was morally justified because it stopped a massacre, and efforts were made to carve out an exception to the U.N. rules, so that a "humanitarian intervention" would be lawful even without Security Council approval. That effort failed because people believed it would be too easy for countries to use humanitarian intervention as a pretext for attacking countries for other reasons. After all, humanitarian conditions are bad in nearly all countries that someone might like to invade. Instead, an international conference hammered together a compromise that all countries have a "Responsibility to Protect" their own citizens and citizens of other countries. But this idea was never sanctified in a treaty and is not law.

The most honest thing to do would be to admit that the international law on the use of force is defunct, as professor Michael Glennon has argued. Virtually all major countries have broken the rules from time to time, even the saintly European countries that joined in the Kosovo intervention. The U.S. has ignored the U.N. rules on numerous occasions— Vietnam [1962-1971], Grenada [1983], Panama [1989], Kosovo [1998], the second Iraq War [2003], and the 2011 war in Libya, where it secured an authorization to stop massacres of civilians but violated its terms by seeking regime change. But the U.S. government does not repudiate the U.N. rules because it wants *other* countries to comply with them.

The Role of Congress

On the domestic front, things are hardly better. The Constitution gives Congress, not the executive, the power to declare war, and at present writing, the administration seems unlikely to ask Congress for authorization lest it say no. This too would be a repeat of the Libya intervention, which lacked congressional authorization. To avoid the impression that the president can go to war whenever he wants, pretty much in clear violation of the founders' intentions, the executive branch has invented a number of largely phony limits on executive military action. At one point the theory was that the executive may send military forces anywhere in the world in order to discharge its responsibility to protect Americans or American property, a theory that was used to justify the use of military force without congressional authorization in Somalia in 1992–1993. One might wonder whether such a theory imposes any limits; one might ask, "In what country are there no Americans or American property that could be protected?" Syria, it turns out.

Laws governing war make us feel more secure but they don't actually make us more secure.

No one alleges that the Syrian government poses a threat to Americans or American property, so the Obama administration can't fall back on that theory, and doesn't seem inclined to. But the executive branch claims the authority to use military intervention to protect the "national interest," and it is not hard to find a national interest at stake. Ironically, the Justice Department's Libya opinion identified "maintaining the credibility of the United Nations Security Council and the effectiveness of its actions to promote international peace and security" as one of the national interests justifying military intervention without congressional approval. Don't expect a repeat of *that* argument in the Syria opinion. The other national interest was that of promoting regional stability—also not a good one here either, since no one seems to think that lobbing some cruise missiles onto Syrian soil will promote regional stability. Most likely the government will argue that there is a (heretofore ignored) national interest in deterring the use of chemical weapons as well as in protecting foreign civilians from massacres. With "national interest" so capaciously understood, it is clear that the president will always be able to find a national interest justifying a military intervention, so there are no constitutional constraints on his power to initiate military intervention.

Congress tried to bring the executive under control back in 1973 by enacting the War Powers Resolution, which can be read to implicitly authorize the use of military force as long as the president reports back to Congress and withdraws forces after 60 days unless Congress gives authorization in the interim. In 2011, President Obama ignored a Justice Department opinion that he must end the use of force in Libya, instead obtaining a compliant legal opinion from White House Counsel Robert Bauer and State Department Legal Adviser Harold Koh, who argued that the bombings and killings in Libya did not amount to "hostilities" and so did not trigger the withdrawal provision in the War Powers Resolution. In another indication of the administration's respect for Congress, earlier this month [August 2013] the administration refused to call the coup in Egypt a coup so as to evade a statute that requires a cutoff of foreign aid to countries in which a military coup overthrows a democratically elected leader.

One can be cynical or realistic. I prefer the latter. The Romans had it right: It is not realistic to put legal constraints on war powers. Law works through general prospective rules that apply to a range of factual situations. International relations and national security are too fluid and unpredictable to be governed by a set of legal propositions that command general assent secured in advance. Laws governing war make us feel more secure but they don't actually make us more secure. So while it is satisfying to fling the charge of hypocrisy at the president and his lawyers, and we might disagree about the wisdom of an attack on Syria, let's just hope that when they invoke the law, they don't actually believe what they are saying.

8

Syria's Chemical Weapons Should Not Be Transported or Dismantled at Sea

Kristina Wong

Kristina Wong is a writer based in Washington, DC.

Plans to destroy Syria's chemical weapons at sea are being met with resistance. Weapons of this nature have never been disposed of at sea, it is unclear what other chemical agents may be in the weapons, and other countries have been reluctant to allow the weapons to pass through their borders on their way to open water. Furthermore, there is a strong risk of attack during the process. While officials insist the plan is safe, many scientists remain deeply skeptical.

Chemical weapons experts are criticizing the Defense Department's plan to destroy Syria's chemical arsenal aboard a U.S. vessel in the Mediterranean Sea, a proposal that Pentagon [US military headquarters] officials have described as low-risk.

The plan calls for neutralizing the liquid components of sarin, mustard gas and VX nerve agent via hydrolysis, a technology that has been used for decades to destroy chemical agents in the U.S. and abroad but never at sea.

Problems with Disposal

"There's no precedence. We're all guessing. We're all estimating," said Raymond Zilinskas, director of the Chemical and

Biological Weapons Nonproliferation Program at the James Martin Center for Nonproliferation Studies, who worked as a U.N. [United Nations] biological weapons inspector in Iraq in 1994.

"For example, you don't know if the sarin is pure. The Iraqi sarin was rather impure, and had a lot of contaminants, and we don't know if that's amenable to hydrolysis," said Mr. Zilinskas, a professor at the Monterey Institute of International Studies at Middlebury College.

Under the Pentagon plan, the toxic stockpile would be transported to the Syrian port of Latakia, loaded onto a non-U.S. vessel and shipped to a third country. From there, a U.S. cargo ship would take the arsenal to sea for destruction.

Richard M. Lloyd, a warhead technology consultant at Tesla Laboratories Inc. who tracks weapons being used in Syria, said he has little confidence in the regime's ability to transport the weapons safely.

"The probability that rebels are going to attack is very high," Mr. Lloyd said. "They want to get their hands on them, or destroy something or do something that's not good."

When we're setting some sort of toxic elimination plan, there would have to be risk assessments done of the impact on the people and the environment. Obviously, that's not being done here.

The Pentagon has proposed sending about 60 civilian workers and contractors to the Middle East early next year [2014] to destroy the chemical stockpile. Specialists from the Organization for the Prohibition of Chemical Weapons, which is tasked with overseeing the dismantling of Syria's chemical arms program, would assist in the mission.

The organization has not given formal approval to any plan, but defense officials said its plan likely will be chosen to meet a Dec. 31 [2013] deadline for removing the "priority one" chemical weapons, which are to be destroyed by June [2014].

Defense officials say they would use two mobile hydrolysis units to neutralize the arsenal and would carry spare parts aboard the ship in case the system fails.

Risk Assessment and Cost

Mr. Zilinskas said no risk assessments are being conducted of the plan's impact on people and the environment, as would be done if the chemicals were to be destroyed on land.

"You don't know if there could be an accident and how you would handle it," he said. "In normal conditions, when we're setting some sort of toxic elimination plan, there would have to be risk assessments done of the impact on the people and the environment. Obviously, that's not being done here."

For an operation at sea, the U.S. should conduct a risk assessment with the International Maritime Organization, Mr. Zilinskas said.

A defense official who requested anonymity to discuss the issue freely said that "planning continues for every aspect of the [Department of Defense's] involvement in the joint mission to eliminate Syria's chemical weapons. I do not believe a specific risk assessment is being conducted at this time; however, we are certainly considering and will address all possible risks to safely carry out the mission."

A sea trial is planned for later this month, the official said.

Defense officials said an alternative proposal to incinerate the arsenal would not meet the deadline and likely would have to be carried out on land, which would create political and security issues. Four nations already have refused to allow for the destruction within their borders.

"No country wants these chemical weapons to be transported across their territory," Mr. Zilinskas said.

On Tuesday [December 10, 2013], Croatian Prime Minister Zoran Milanovic said his government is considering participating in the destruction of Syria's chemical arsenal—but only if the public does not oppose it.

If the Organization for the Prohibition of Chemical Weapons approves the Pentagon plan, about 60 civilian defense workers and inspectors would board the U.S. cargo ship *Cape Ray* early next year to destroy the arsenal, which would take 45 to 90 days. The waste byproducts would be disposed of at a commercial treatment facility that has yet to be determined.

No U.S. troops would be aboard the vessel, but the U.S. and its allies will provide security for the ship during its mission. Officials did not offer a cost estimate for the plan, but analysts speculate that it would be as much as $70 million.

The operation's cost would be covered as an "in-kind contribution from the government of the United States," a senior defense official said on the condition of anonymity to discuss the issue.

A U.S.-Russian deal to dismantle Syria's chemical weapons program by mid-2014 averted U.S. plans for military strikes on Syria after the regime used chemical weapons against rebels in August [2013], killing about 1,400 people, including many children.

Officials insist the plan is safe and environmentally sound.

"The chemicals and their reactions are well understood," the senior defense official said. "The Department of Defense has decades of experience in chemical demilitarization programs.

"Absolutely nothing will be dumped at sea," the official added.

Defense officials said the risks are "very low" but acknowledged that transporting the chemicals could be risky, as Syria's civil war enters its third year with no signs of abatement.

"Technically, there are no problems with this plan as long as containers are used that are impervious to chemical weapons—which are often corrosive—and that they are well-packaged under guidelines that the U.S. uses to contain and transport chemical weapons," said a government scientist with knowledge of the plan who requested anonymity to discuss the issue.

"What is happening in the country outside of the containers might be an issue," the scientist said.

Hundreds of tons of chemical agents are stored in about 150 shipping containers that will need to be transported within the war-torn country to Latakia, officials said.

"Obviously, it's a challenging environment," a senior defense official said. "The Syrians are taking the process very seriously. They're working closely with [the Organization for the Prohibition of Chemical Weapons], the U.N. and the joint mission to conduct that part of the operation safely and effectively."

9

The United States Needs to Eliminate Its Own Chemical Weapons Stockpile

Dave Lindorff

Dave Lindorff is an American investigative reporter.

Although the United States requested an extension until 2023 to safely dispose of its chemical weapons stockpile, the country continues to demand that Syria dispose of its weapons in a matter of months or risk military action. Even in the best of situations, disposing of chemical weapons is no small task. For Syria, a developing nation in the middle of a civil war, the task is even more challenging and risky.

The US is demanding, in negotiations at the UN [United Nations], that all Syrian chemical weapons, stocks and production facilities be eliminated by June 30 of next year [2014]. This has an element of hypocrisy, because the US itself has been incredibly slow about eliminating its own stocks of chemical weapons.

US Secretary of State John Kerry has referred to Syria as having one of the largest chemical stockpiles in the world. But the US and Russia both still have stocks of chemicals many times as large. Syria's neighbor Israel, which refuses to admit it has the weapons and has yet to ratify the treaty banning them, is suspected of also having a large arsenal.

The US caches, at 3100 tons, are three times as large as Syria's reported 1000 tons.

Problems with Compliance

The United Nations Convention on Chemical Weapons, which Washington [DC, the nation's capital] ratified in 1997, required signers to eliminate all stocks of chemical arms by 2012. But the US, like Russia, requested an extension to 2023. It claimed that "difficulties involving old chemical warheads" and environmental issues were making it impossible to comply within the framework of the treaty.

Disposing of chemical weapons is not something you just do, like snapping your fingers.

Destroying the stocks is no small task. The Army's Pueblo Chemical Depot, in Pueblo, Colorado, still houses an estimated 2611 tons of mustard gas and the Blue Grass Army Depot, Blue Grass, Kentucky, may have on site 523 tons of sarin (the same weapons whose use in Syria caused such an uproar), VX and mustard gas agent. That's a whole lot of poison to dispose of safely.

Some $10 billion has been spent to date on the process of locating and destroying the US chemical arsenal—and the ultimate cost may top $30 billion. According to the US Army Chemical Materials Agency (USACMA), two mammoth destruction facilities are being constructed, at a cost of billions of dollars each, at the Pueblo and Blue Grass sites, by the notorious war profiteer corporation Bechtel Parsons.

In other words, disposing of chemical weapons is not something you just do, like snapping your fingers.

Worse, some experts suspect the US of the exact same fakeout game it accuses Syria of contemplating.

Meryl Nass, a physician with the group Physicians for Social Responsibility, who since 2007 has run a respected blog about biological and chemical weapons called Anthrax Vaccine is wary of reports from USACMA about accidental leaks of sarin gas. "I'm concerned that this could be a cover for removing some stocks from the accounting and the destruction process," Nass says, "so that UN inspectors can be told that the missing material had simply leaked away."

Even in the purportedly safest, most stable settings, like those US sites, destroying chemicals and poison gas is a tricky proposition, with vast environmental, health and safety risks. After all, these substances can kill hundreds of people in short order if anything goes wrong. But such concerns surely must be multiplied ten-fold when the same process is being undertaken in a civil war environment in a third-world country such as Syria.

Yet the US is insisting that Syria's gas stocks must be gone or destroyed within the next eight and a half months. If that doesn't happen, says Washington, the UN Security Council should sign off on a military campaign. As further backup, the US is still prepared to act unilaterally with a punitive bombing and rocket blitz against the Syrian government's forces.

That impatience is astonishing when one considers that the US itself says it needs *over a quarter of a century* to destroy its own chemical arsenal. That's because it wants to construct those two expensive state-of-the-art chemical weapons destruction facilities, ostensibly for safety reasons (though presumably pork barrel politics plays a role). And it plans to take its time. The Army says the facility in Pueblo won't begin operation until 2017, and the one in Blue Grass won't even be ready for operation until 2020.

Another reason some are skeptical about the US's intentions is that notwithstanding this long-term proposition, the US admits it already possesses and has in the past used mobile truck-mounted destruction equipment capable of destroying five tons of toxic weapons per day. Do the math: at this rate the entire US stockpile could be eliminated in less than *two* years—that's 2015, a far cry from the current target date of 2023.

A BBC report says these US mobile destruction units, each called an Explosive Destruction System, work by putting chemical warheads or shells into a "bang box" and exploding them, thus neutralizing the warhead and the toxin. Each unit is capable of destroying six weapons at a time. These units were reportedly used to destroy "more than 1700 items" in the US arsenal since 2001.

But they are no longer being used. Why—is not clear.

Environmental Safety Concerns

The army ascribes these lengthy delays to environmental concerns.

Miguel Monteverde, a spokesman for the Program Executive Office, Assembled Chemical Weapons Alternatives, the Army department responsible for overseeing the destruction of the remaining US chemical arms, tells *WhoWhatWhy* that the snails' pace should be ascribed to worries expressed by residents of the Pueblo and Blue Grass communities.

Monteverde says that in response to local sentiment, the army scrapped initial plans to incinerate most of the remaining weapons (the method used to destroy most of the other 28,000 tons of US chemical weapons already eliminated), and new facilities were planned that will use "safer" methods.

Many of America's stockpiled weapons contain deadly toxins linked to explosive warheads or potentially explosive propulsion systems that could be triggered inadvertently.

The new plants, he said, will also be "fully automated" so that no human hands will have to handle the deadly weapons and chemicals. Yet the army rep concedes that during the destruction of 90% of the US arsenal in prior decades there was "not one fatality" among workers.

As for those mobile Pentagon units, which were designed following 9–11 [2001] for use in case a terrorist stash of chemical or biological weapons was discovered, Monteverde says they are "not appropriate" for the job of eliminating the remaining stocks. "There's too much risk because people have to handle the weapons," he explained.

That of course begs the question of what risks would be posed to those—most likely Syrians hired by any UN-led team charged with destroying Syria's chemical weapons—if the process were done in a hurry and "under the gun" of US threats of bombardment.

Many of America's stockpiled weapons contain deadly toxins linked to explosive warheads or potentially explosive propulsion systems that could be triggered inadvertently. If this makes deactivating them so difficult it's taking the US a generation to accomplish, can we really expect an ad hoc international team to eliminate Syria's weapons in only eight months—in the midst of a horrific civil war?

These would seem the core questions to be asked about this raging international issue. But few are asking them.

Chemical Versus Cluster Weapons

There is one other big issue that suggests a double standard.

While the US decries Syria's alleged use of chemical weapons "against its own people" in the Aug. 21 [2013] incident in a Damascus suburb, the United States itself is a holdout (along with Russia, China, Israel, Syria and Pakistan) and an active opponent of another UN convention, which went into force in 2008. It bans anti-personnel cluster weapons. These insidious devices have killed and maimed far more people than poison gas in the years since World War I. And since World War II the primary user of these nightmarish weapons has been the US.

Indeed, it is likely that the Tomahawk cruise missile blitz that the [Barack] Obama administration came close to launching against Syrian government installations and military targets in late summer—and which it still wants to keep as an open threat—would have included cluster weapons. For they are among the warheads designed for use on the Tomahawk.

Missile-delivered cluster weapons are notorious for their imprecision, with as many as 98% of their victims proving to be civilians. President Obama, in his Sept. 10 [2013] address to the nation on Syria's chemical weapons, made much of the tragic images of children allegedly dying from Syrian government poison gas weapons in Damascus.

But in trying to make the case for a Tomahawk attack on Syria, the President ignored the reality that fully 40% of the victims of cluster weapons, which the US has used massively in Iraq, Afghanistan and even in Yemen, are children.

10

Israel's Chemical Weapons Are a Bigger Threat to Peace than Syria's

Stephen Lendman

Stephen Lendman is a blogger and the author of several books, including Banker Occupation: Waging Financial War on Humanity.

Israel, armed with nuclear, chemical, and biological weapons, is a global threat. Very little information about its stockpile, research and development, or use makes it to media outlets because whistleblowers are imprisoned and the storage areas are heavily secured. While Syria is under international pressure to eliminate its weapons stockpile, Israel has been given free reign to continue its program.

Syria threatens no one. It hasn't used chemical weapons against insurgents or its own civilians. Claims otherwise are fabricated.

In contrast, Israel is nuclear armed and dangerous. It maintains large chemical and biological weapons arsenals. More on that below.

In 1986, Dimona [Israel] nuclear technician/heroic whistleblower Mordechai Vanunu revealed important documents, photos, and other scientific evidence.

Israel's Weapons

They proved Israel began producing atomic weapons since at least the 1960s. Years later, thermonuclear warheads were manufactured.

It's believed Israel's arsenal includes hundreds it won't admit to publicly. It's missile capability can deliver them long range. So can its nuclear submarines.

Vanunu revealed Israel's nuclear program. He provided credible evidence. Doing so cost him dearly.

In 1986, Mossad [Israeli intelligence agency] agents lured him to Rome. They beat, drugged and kidnapped him. He was secretly tried. He was convicted on espionage and treason charges.

He got 18 years in prison. He spent much of it in brutalizing solitary confinement. He suffered cruel and barbaric treatment.

After release, he was imprisoned again. It was for speaking to foreign journalists. Daniel Ellsberg [former US military analyst who released top-secret Pentagon Papers] calls him "the preeminent hero of the nuclear era."

Vanunu said "I am neither a traitor nor a spy. I only wanted the world to know what was happening." People everywhere have a right to know.

Vanunu's prohibited from leaving Israel. His fundamental rights are denied. He received numerous Nobel Peace Prize nominations.

Israel denies him freedom. It's for doing the right thing. He, Edward Snowden [US government computer contractor who leaked US National Security Agency information], Bradley Manning [US Army soldier who leaked US military secrets through WikiLeaks], and other heroic whistleblowers deserve universal acclaim.

Instead they're ruthlessly vilified, hounded and punished when apprehended. Snowden's free in Russia. He's unable to go home. He fears for his safety.

No matter how secure he is in Russia or elsewhere, he's threatened for the rest of his life. "There's no saving me," he says. It's for good reason.

Israel won't discuss its weapons of mass destruction.

Perhaps Mossad will try to abduct him. It wouldn't surprise if it attempts replicating how it entrapped Vanunu. Rogue agencies operate this way.

CIA [Central Intelligence Agency], NSA [National Security Agency], Mossad and Israel's secretive Unit 8200 perhaps are the worst. They operate extrajudicially. They make their own rules. They've done it throughout their history. Returning Snowden to America very much is US policy.

Israel Not Party to WMD Agreements

Israel won't discuss its weapons of mass destruction. It never signed the Nuclear Non-Proliferation Treaty (NPT).

In 1993, it signed the Chemical Weapons Convention (CWC). It refused to ratify it. It did so for spurious reasons. It wrongfully claims it's surrounded by hostile neighbors. Israel's only enemies are ones it invents.

It never signed the 1972 Biological Weapons Convention (BWC). Its policy is CBW [chemical and biological weapons] ambiguity.

In 1993, the US Congress Office of Technology Assessment WMD proliferation assessment said Israel has undeclared offensive chemical warfare capabilities.

It uses banned weapons in all its conflicts. They include chemical, biological, and radiological ones. Hideous new weapons are tested. Injuries never seen before are reported.

Bodies with dead tissue showed no apparent wounds. Corpses were found shrunken. Civilians had heavy lower limb damage. Amputations were required.

Internal wounds had no trace of shrapnel. Corpses were blackened. They weren't burned. Some badly wounded victims didn't bleed. Explosives containing toxins and radiological materials are used.

They burn and destroy bodies. They do so internally. They leave permanent deformations. Unknown toxins believed to be nerve gas is used. So is white phosphorous. It burns flesh to the bone.

Depleted and enriched uranium weapons spread radioactive contamination. Close-range explosives cause severe injuries. Victims lose legs. Abdomens are sliced open. Some people are too far gone to be saved.

The Israeli Institute for Biological Research (IIBR) is top secret. Hundreds of scientists and technicians develop chemical and biological weapons. They're used in combat.

Its publications discuss research on various agents and toxins. They include plague bacterium (Yersinia pestis), typhus bacterium (Rickettsia prowazekii), staphylococcal enterotoxin B (SEB), rabies, anthrax bacterium (Bacillus anthracis), botulinum bacterium (Clostridium botulinum), botulinum toxin, Ebola virus, and nerve gas agents like sarin.

In terms of life science capability, Israel's ranks among the world's most expert nations in biology, chemistry, biochemistry, molecular biology, genetics, neuroscience, and clinical medicine.

Its biotechnological expertise is sophisticated and innovative. Its bioscience infrastructure is modern and well-funded. It provides what experts call "breakout" capability. Its activities are top secret.

Official policy prohibits discussing anything related to Israel's nuclear, chemical or biological programs. Doing so is considered treason. Vanunu learned the hard way. It didn't diminish his passion to expose important truths.

IIBR works closely with Israeli military and intelligence operations. Strategic priorities are agreed on. They relate to what Israel wants for combat use.

On September 9, [2013] *Foreign Policy* headlined "Exclusive: Does Israel Have Chemical Weapons Too?"

Sorting Through the Evidence

According to 1982 CIA documents, US satellites uncovered "a probable CW [chemical weapon] nerve agent production facility and a storage facility."

It's located at the Dimona Sensitive Storage Area in the Negev desert. Other CW production is believed to exist within "a well-developed Israeli chemical industry."

Evidence of Israeli chemical, biological and radiological weapons development [was uncovered] decades ago.

"While (CIA) cannot confirm whether the Israelis possess lethal chemical agents, several indicators lead (it) to believe that they have available to them at least persistent and non-persistent nerve agents, a mustard agent, and several riot-control agents, matched with suitable delivery systems."

What existed decades earlier is likely far more expansive and sophisticated now. Israel doesn't develop expertise to abandon it.

CIA intelligence uncovered evidence of Israeli chemical, biological and radiological weapons development decades ago.

Nothing is reported publicly. *Foreign Policy* (FP) said an unnamed researcher found an "innocuous unclassified report."

It was dated September 15, 1983. It was titled "Implications of Soviet Use of Chemical and Toxin Weapons for US Security Interests."

It dealt mainly with unproven allegations of Soviet chemical and biological weapons use in Afghanistan and Southeast Asia.

It included "unredacted portions of the intelligence estimate that details what the CIA thought it knew back in 1983 about Israel's work on chemical weapons."

It revealed "hard evidence that Israel possessed a chemical weapons stockpile of indeterminate size, including, according to the report, 'persistent and non-persistent nerve agents.'"

It was believed virtually for sure to be sarin. In 1988, Israeli historian Avner Cohen's book titled *Israel and the Bomb* said Prime Minister David Ben-Gurion secretly ordered developing chemical weapons.

He did so in the mid-1950s. CIA intelligence indicates years later. According to its 1983 estimate:

"Israel, finding itself surrounded by frontline Arab states with budding CW capabilities, became increasingly conscious of its vulnerability to chemical attack."

"Its sensitivities were galvanized by the capture of large quantities of Soviet CW-related equipment during both the 1967 Arab-Israeli and the 1973 Yom Kippur wars."

"As a result, Israel undertook a program of chemical warfare preparations in both offensive and protective areas."

CIA officials first learned about Israel's chemical weapons in the early 1970s, said FP. It discovered test grids for them.

They're specially instrumented areas. They're used to measure the range and effectiveness of different chemical agents.

They include nerve agents like sarin. They're tested in simulated situations. It's done under varying climate conditions. Israel did so secretly in barren Negev desert areas.

Following the 1973 Yom Kippur War, CIA intelligence said Israel accelerated its program.

NSA spied on Israel. It still does. It intercepted communications showing Israeli fighter-bombers conducted simulated low-level chemical weapons delivery missions. They did so at a Negev bombing range.

At the same time, Israel's nuclear arsenal grew "both in size and raw megatonnage." CIA officials were quoted saying Israel has sophisticated nuclear weapons.

It's actively engaged in developing other weapons of mass destruction. Further elaboration didn't follow.

In 1982, US spy satellite evidence showed "a probable CW nerve agent production facility and a storage facility."

It discovered them at the Dimona Sensitive Storage Area. It's based in the Negev desert. It's in a virtually uninhabited area. It's located east of al-Kilab village.

Whatever Israel had [in 1982] is likely far more expansive and sophisticated now. Evidence from Israel's wars on Palestine and Lebanon suggests so.

It's 10 miles west of Dimona. It's heavily protected. It includes 50 buried bunkers. They're surrounded by double barbed wire fencing. Large-scale security forces are present.

Two miles northeast, another complex is heavily guarded. It's protected the same way. It covers about 40 or 50 acres.

It consists of three large storage bunkers. It includes a buried production and/or maintenance facility. It may be where Israel produces sarin and/or other nerve agents.

Whatever Israel had then is likely far more expansive and sophisticated now. Evidence from Israel's wars on Palestine and Lebanon suggests so.

According to FP, "Israel has a well-known penchant for preserving any asset thought to be needed for (its) defense regardless of the cost or possible diplomatic ramifications."

Israeli policy reflects do what we say, not what we do. On September 11 [2013], [prime minister of Israel Benjamin] Netanyahu wrongfully accused Syria of using chemical weapons against its own people.

Syria Is Not a Threat

"We must make sure that the Syrian regime is stripped of its chemical weapons, and the world must make sure that whoever uses weapons of mass destruction pays a price for it," he said.

He ignored his own government's culpability. He ignored crimes of numerous Israeli leaders preceding him.

"The message that is received in Syria will be received loudly in Iran," he added.

Israel refuses to sign NPT. It never ratified CWC. It won't permit international inspections. It operates lawlessly. It does so covertly. Washington and other Western states turn a blind eye.

They do so despite Israel's global threat. They wrongfully focus on Syria and Iran. Both nations threaten no one. Claims otherwise are fabricated.

Iran was one of NPT's first signatories. It ratified CWC. Syria ratified NPT. It pledged signing and ratifying CWC.

Israel's a nuclear, chemical, and biological weapons outlaw. Syria promises full compliance with international treaties, conventions and protocols.

It's wrongfully targeted. It's shamelessly accused of numerous insurgent crimes. They include chemical weapons attacks, numerous massacres, and gruesome atrocities.

World leaders point fingers the wrong way. They let Israel get away with murder. They do so repeatedly.

They're complicit in Israel's worst crimes of war and against humanity. Don't expect them on the right side of history ahead.

They're allied with Washington against [Syrian president Bashar al-]Assad. They want Syrian sovereignty destroyed. They want pro-Western subservient governance replacing it. They want Iran isolated.

[Barack] Obama wants war. Russia's peace initiative slowed him. He's not deterred. His war plans are unchanged. He could initiate them any time.

It could happen sooner than expected. Doing so may be one more major false flag away. Reports suggest one targeting Israel.

Perhaps Obama's conspiring with Netanyahu and insurgent fighters to launch it. For sure bombs away would follow.

11

The Inconsistent US Role on Chemical Weapons

Stephen Zunes

Stephen Zunes is a professor of politics and international studies at the University of San Francisco.

The US policy on chemical weapons is inconsistent. Although the United States threatened in 2013 to strike Syria if it didn't relinquish its weapons, the government has never made the same request of either Israel or Egypt. This is despite the fact that Egypt has engaged in chemical warfare, and Israel is believed to have an advanced chemical weapons program. The United States also aided Iraq in using chemical weapons against Iran during the 1980s. The United States should maintain a consistent policy against chemical weapons.

The Syrian regime's apparent use of chemical weapons against civilian areas Aug. 21 constitutes a major breach of the Geneva Protocol of 1925, one of the world's most important disarmament treaties, which banned the use of chemical weapons. The Obama administration has made clear that the only way the Syrian regime could avoid U.S. military strikes on their country would be to place their chemical weapons stockpiles under international control to ensure their removal and destruction, which is now underway as a result of the U.N. Security Council resolution passed unanimously Sept. 27.

Stephen Zunes, "The Inconsistent US Role on Chemical Weapons," *National Catholic Reporter*, October 28, 2013. Copyright © 2013 by National Catholic Reporter. Reprinted by permission of National Catholic Reporter, 115 E Armour Blvd, Kansas City, MO 64111. www.ncronline.org.

In 1993, the international community ratified the Chemical Weapons Convention, a binding international treaty that would prohibit the development, production, acquisition, stockpiling, retention and transfer or use of chemical weapons. An outgrowth of the convention is the Organization for the Prohibition of Chemical Weapons, which has successfully overseen the destruction of more than 80 percent of the world's chemical weapons over the past 20 years. A joint U.N.-OPCW team arrived in Syria Oct. 1 to oversee the elimination of Syria's chemical weapons production facilities.

The Obama administration's support for OPCW stands in contrast to the Bush administration, which was dismissive of the agency and forced the removal of its highly effective chairman José Bustani in 2002.

Syria is one of only eight of the world's 193 countries not party to the Chemical Weapons Convention. Neither are the world's two largest recipients of U.S. military aid—Israel and Egypt—which is just one example of the United States' inconsistent and politicized policy regarding chemical weapons. No Congress nor any administration of either party has ever called on Israel or Egypt to disarm their chemical weapons arsenals, much less threatened war for their failure to do so.

During the Iran-Iraq War in the 1980s, Saddam Hussein used chemical weapons on a scale far greater than any country had dared since their banning following World War I.

It's not as if Syria is the only country that has engaged in chemical warfare. Egypt used phosgene and mustard gas in the mid-1960s during its intervention in Yemen's civil war. The U.S.-backed Egyptian regime has continued its chemical weapons research and development program.

Israel is widely believed to have produced and stockpiled an extensive range of chemical weapons and to be engaged in ongoing research and development of additional chemical weaponry. Indeed, it appears that Syria may have initiated its chemical weapons program as a response to Israel's chemical, biological and nuclear programs.

During the Iran-Iraq War in the 1980s, Saddam Hussein used chemical weapons on a scale far greater than any country had dared since their banning following World War I. The Iraqis inflicted close to 100,000 casualties among Iranian soldiers using banned chemical agents, resulting in 20,000 deaths and tens of thousands of long-term injuries.

They were unable to do this alone, however. Despite ongoing Iraqi support for Abu Nidal and other terrorist groups during the 1980s, the Reagan administration removed Iraq from the State Department's list of state sponsors of terrorism to provide the regime with thiodiglycol, a key component in the manufacture of mustard gas, and other chemical precursors for their weapons program. In fact, recently released CIA documents show that personnel from the U.S. Defense Intelligence Agency were dispatched to Baghdad during the war to provide Saddam's regime with U.S. satellite data on the location of Iranian troop concentrations in the full knowledge that the Iraqis were using chemical weapons against them.

Even the Iraqi regime's use of chemical weapons against civilians was not seen as particularly problematic.

The Reagan administration downplayed Saddam's massacre of up to 5,000 Kurdish civilians with chemical weapons in the northern Iraqi city of Halabja in March 1988. Some officials even falsely claimed that Iran was actually responsible. The United States continued sending aid to Iraq even after the regime's use of poison gas was confirmed. Both the Reagan and George H.W. Bush administrations blocked congressional efforts to place sanctions on the Iraqi regime in response to the chemical weapons attacks.

After denying and covering up Iraq's use of chemical weapons in the late 1980s, the U.S. government—first under Presi-

dent Bill Clinton and then under President George W. Bush—
then began insisting that Iraq's alleged chemical weapons
stockpile was a dire threat, even though the country had completely destroyed its stockpile by 1993 and dismantled its
chemical weapons program.

This year, Secretary of State John Kerry led the Obama
administration's initial efforts to convince Congress to authorize military force against Syria by insisting, "Chemical weapons were used by the regime. We know this." However, in the
fall of 2002, Sen. Kerry falsely claimed, "Iraq has chemical and
biological weapons . . . and [their weapons programs] are
larger and more advanced than they were before the Gulf
War."

Similarly, House Democratic leader Nancy Pelosi, who led
the pro-war effort in that chamber, insisted that Syria's use of
chemical weapons is "undeniable." However, in November
2002, she falsely claimed that Iraq "certainly" had chemical
weapons and that there was "no question about that."

Even though they are apparently telling the truth this
time, this record of deceit makes it difficult to trust U.S. officials when it comes to accusations regarding hostile Arab gov-
ernments and chemical weapons.

Even more problematic has been U.S. efforts to block
region-wide efforts at disarmament.

U.N. Security Council Resolution 687, the resolution
passed at the end of the 1991 Gulf War demanding the destruction of Iraq's chemical and biological weapons and the
dismantling of its nuclear program, also called on member
states "to work towards the establishment in the Middle East
of a zone free of such weapons."

Syria has joined virtually all other Arab states in calling
for such a "weapons of mass destruction-free zone" for the
entire Middle East. In December 2003, Syria introduced a

U.N. Security Council resolution reiterating this clause from 12 years earlier, but the resolution was tabled as a result of a threatened U.S. veto.

A case can be made, then, that had the United States pursued a policy that addressed the proliferation of nonconventional weapons through region-wide disarmament rather than trying to single out Syria, the Syrian regime would have rid itself of its chemical weapons some years earlier, along with Israel and Egypt, and the tragic use of such ordnance and the resulting push toward war would have never happened.

12

Chemical Weapons Are Morally Worse than Conventional Weapons

Tom Blackwell

Tom Blackwell is a health-care reporter with the National Post.

Both chemical weapons and conventional weapons have the power to cause suffering and death. But chemical weapons are seen as uniquely immoral because they kill indiscriminately and without warning, have the potential for a far greater number of casualties than conventional weapons, and are easier for terrorists to obtain. Chemical weapons have the potential to create disasters on a scale larger than any the world has yet seen, and their creation, storage, and use should be banned.

In little more than two years, the Syrian civil war has distinguished itself as a particularly vicious conflict.

The United Nations estimates conservatively that more than 100,000 people have died, including thousands of women and children, with civilians often directly targeted or killed in indiscriminate assaults.

The [Syrian president Bashar al-]Assad regime has deployed an array of nasty weapons, from cluster bombs to napalm-like incendiary devices and thermobaric explosives,

Tom Blackwell, "The Immoral, Silent Killer: Why Chemical Warfare Instills in People a Fear that Conventional Attacks Do Not," *National Post*, August 30, 2013. Material reprinted with the express permission of: National Post, a division of Postmedia Network, Inc.

whose blast of pressure and heat incinerates anyone at the impact site—and vacuums the air out of the lungs of people nearby.

Yet it was a singular event just last week that rallied the West into its most concerted response yet to the hostilities. Only after the Aug. 21 [2013] attack with suspected nerve gas, killing an estimated 350 to 1,400 men, women and children, did the U.S. and others talk seriously—for better or worse—of military intervention.

The reaction reflects a long-held view of chemical weapons as an essentially immoral way to wage war, with efforts to ban them internationally being made as long ago as the 19th century and President Barack Obama declaring their use his "red line" in Syria.

But after so much Syrian bloodshed, the sudden uptick in concern raises awkward questions: Why is there such revulsion to chemical warfare specifically? Is it so much worse than the other ways armed forces can kill, disfigure and terrorize?

What Makes Chemical Weapons Unique?

Experts agree there is an existential fear of chemical attacks, partly rooted in the horrific ordeal of gassed soldiers in the First World War, and warn they must be discouraged to avoid far worse atrocities.

Still, some argue that as a mechanism of death, chemical weapons may be unmatched in their emotional impact, but not really in physical cruelty.

"We respond in a very emotional way, in a subjective way," said Charles Blair, a senior fellow at the Federation of American Scientists.

"They couldn't smell it, see it coming and 'wham,' next thing you know they're in convulsions, frothing at the mouth and they're dead. It's terrible—but no more terrible than all the other wars."

The world was undeniably riveted, though, by the attack in Syria, documented with chilling images of children who died at the hands of an invisible, intangible enemy.

Nerve agents such as sarin likely cause less suffering than the chlorine and mustard gases of the First World War, but are more efficient at killing, and therein may lie their true menace.

An 1899 treaty banned "asphyxiating or deleterious gases," though the United States refused to sign on.

One suitcase-sized artillery shell loaded with sarin could wipe out the occupants of an entire football stadium, said Michael Luhan of the Organization for the Prohibition of Chemical Weapons.

"They have become weapons of terror," he said. "You put yourself in a position where you're in your neighbourhood and suddenly, without knowing anything, without smelling anything, seeing anything, people's eyes bug out, they start gasping for breath and hyper-ventilating, going into convulsions. You don't know what the hell's going on."

Chemical weapons—and the fear of them—are certainly not new, with evidence from ancient times even of chemical attacks.

An 1899 treaty banned "asphyxiating or deleterious gases," though the United States refused to sign on.

It was during the First World War the issue came to the forefront, though, with Canadians playing an historic role. The first troops from this country to see action in Europe were sideswiped by the Germans' first-ever use of chlorine gas—April 22, 1915, on the outskirts of the Belgian town of Ypres.

The gas causes fluid build-up in the lungs, an effect likened to drowning.

"When it came along towards us it turned green, a greeny-yellow colour," recalled infantryman Lester Stevens in an interview preserved by Archives Canada.

"Two fellows, one on my right and one on my left dropped and eventually they got them to hospital but they both died."

Wilfred Owen, the British war poet, describes in his most famous work a chlorine-gassed soldier, with blood "gargling from the froth-corrupted lungs."

The Germans later expanded their arsenal with mustard gas, a blistering agent that burns skin and lungs, and the Allies responded with their own chemical weapons.

Another effort to ban such methods came with 1925's Geneva Protocol.

But it did not stop Japanese, Italian and Egyptian forces using them from the 1930s to 1960s. Chemical agents reappeared on the battlefields of the Iran-Iraq War, and were used by Iraq's [dictator] Saddam Hussein to kill 5,000 civilians in the Kurdish village of Halabja in 1988.

The Chemical Weapons Convention again banned their use in 1997, with all but Syria and six other countries signing. It has led to 85% of the world's stockpile being destroyed, "unprecedented in the annals of arms control," said Mr. Luhan, whose agency oversees the treaty.

Concern for the Future

Most of the world retains a "hard-wired" fear of a weapon that not only is indiscriminate but, especially in the form of the newest agents, can kill in minutes without the victim hearing, seeing, feeling or smelling the gas, said Mr. Blair.

While explosives, bullets and napalm can cause lingering, painful death, they often also bring instant demise. Chemical agents are never so clean, representing "a particularly horrible way of killing people," argued Gavin Cameron, a political scientist and expert on weapons of mass destruction at the University of Calgary.

And yet, did what happened to those children in Syria really represent a greater horror than others in war? Stan Brown, a chemistry professor and chemical weapons expert at Queen's University in Kingston, Ont. [Ontario, Canada], is not so sure.

"Turn the leaf over in the newspaper and you see a bomb blast in central Baghdad and it kills 50 people and injures dozens more," he said.

"That is equally as abhorrent, but I think we've become used to that kind of thing . . . because we see so much of blasts and bombing and shell fire and bullets."

In fact, people likely die more quickly and in less pain from sarin poisoning than if they bled to death from a shrapnel wound, Mr. Blair said.

Perhaps the most compelling reason to treat chemicals as a line that must not be crossed is their potential, at least, to create disasters far worse than any we have seen.

Some analysts also argue Western nations can easily condemn their use because their militaries depend on different tools.

"Powerful countries like the United States cultivate a taboo against using [weapons of mass destruction] partly because they have a vast advantage in conventional arms," wrote political scientist Dominic Tierney on *The Atlantic* magazine website recently.

Mr. Luhan counters there is now a rare, widespread international consensus [that] chemical weapons are abhorrent. The world must ensure those advances don't start sliding back in the outskirts of Damascus, said the chemical disarmament organization's spokesman.

Perhaps the most compelling reason to treat chemicals as a line that must not be crossed is their potential, at least, to create disasters far worse than any we have seen.

The 1995 sarin attack on a Tokyo subway by Aum Shin-rikya terrorists, which killed 13 commuters and injured hundreds of others, hinted at the more widespread horrors the weapons could inflict in the hands of terrorists or rogue states, said Jim Lewis of the Center for Arms Control & Non-Proliferation in Washington.

Large volumes of sarin or other nerve agents dispersed in enclosed spaces would cause "massive" casualties, he said.

"There's not a high technological barrier to making these," echoed Mr. Luhan. "They are the poor man's weapon of mass destruction."

13

Chemical Weapons Are Not Morally Worse than Conventional Weapons

Mike LaBossiere

Mike LaBossiere is a philosophy professor at Florida A&M University, blogger, and author of numerous articles, as well as the book What Don't You Know?

While the United States has taken a stand against Syria's use of chemical weapons, there is nothing inherently worse about the use of chemical weapons over conventional ones. While chemical weapons may be more feared because the effects are thought to be particularly horrific, conventional weapons have the same end result. Both chemical and conventional weapons are used to kill people and both can cause suffering—neither one is worse than the other.

While the Syrian government has been condemned for killing people with conventional weapons, the "red line" drawn by President [Barack] Obama was the use of weapons of mass destruction, specifically chemical weapons. Those more cynical than I might suggest that this amounted to saying "we do not like that you are slaughtering people, but as long as you use conventional weapons . . . well, we will not do much beyond condemning you."

While the Syrian government seemed content with conventional weapons, it has been claimed that government forces

Mike LaBossiere, "Chemical Weapons & Ethics," *Talking Philosophy*, September 2, 2013.

used chemical weapons. Fortunately, Secretary of State John Kerry did not use the phrase "slam dunk" when describing the matter. As this is being written [September 2013], President Obama has stated that he wants to launch an attack on Syria, but he has decided to let congress make the decision. While this raises some interesting issues, I will focus on the question of whether chemical weapons change the ethics of the situation. In more general terms, the issue is whether or not chemical weapons are morally worse than conventional weapons.

Chemical Weapons Perceived as Worse

In terms of general perception, chemical weapons are often regarded with more fear and disgust than conventional weapons. Part of this is historical in nature. World War I saw the first large scale deployment of chemical weapons (primarily gas launched via artillery shells). While conventional artillery and machine guns did the bulk of the killing, gas attacks were regarded with a special horror. One reason was that the effects of gas tended to be rather awful, even compared to the wounds that could be inflicted by conventional weapons. This history of chemical weapons still seems to influence us today.

Conventional weapons, such as bombs and artillery, can inflict horrific wounds that can rival the suffering inflicted by chemical weapons.

Another historically based reason, I suspect, is the ancient view that the use of poison is inherently evil or at least cowardly. In both history and literature, poisoners are rarely praised and are typically cast as villains. Even in games, such as Dungeons & Dragons, the use of poison is regarded as an inherently evil act. In contrast, killing someone with a sword or gun can be acceptable (and even heroic).

A third historically based reason is, of course, the use of poison gas by the Nazis in their attempt to implement their final solution. This would obviously provide the use of poison gas with a rather evil connection.

Of course, these historical explanations are just that—explanations. They provide reasons as to why people psychologically regard such weapons as worse than conventional weapons. What is needed is evidence for one side or the other.

Another part of this is that chemical weapons (as mentioned above) often have awful effects. That is, they do not merely kill—they inflict terrible suffering. This, then, does provide an actual reason as to why chemical weapons might be morally worse than conventional weapons. The gist of the reasoning is that while killing is generally bad, the method of killing does matter. As such, the greater suffering inflicted by chemical weapons makes them morally worse than conventional weapons.

Conventional Weapons

There are three obvious replies to this. The first is that conventional weapons, such as bombs and artillery, can inflict horrific wounds that can rival the suffering inflicted by chemical weapons. The second is that chemical weapons can be designed so that they kill quickly and with minimal suffering. If the moral distinction is based on the suffering of the targets, then such chemical weapons would be morally superior to conventional weapons. However, it is worth noting that horrific chemical weapons would thus be worse than less horrific conventional (or chemical) weapons.

The third is that wrongfully killing and wounding people with conventional weapons would still be evil. Even if it is assumed that chemical weapons are somewhat worse in the suffering they inflict, it would seem that the moral red line should be the killing of people rather than killing them with chemical weapons. After all, the distinction between not killing people and killing them seems far greater than the distinction between killing people with conventional weapons and killing them with chemical weapons. For example, having soldiers machine gun everyone in a village seems to be morally as bad as having soldiers fire gas shells onto the village until everyone is dead. After all, the results are the same.

Another aspect of chemical weapons that supposedly makes them worse than conventional weapons is that they are claimed to be indiscriminate. For example, a chemical weapon is typically deployed as a gas and the gas can drift and spread into areas outside of the desired target. As another example, some chemical agents are persistent—they remain dangerous for some time after the initial attack and thus can harm and kill those who were not the intended targets. This factor certainly seems morally relevant.

The obvious reply is that conventional weapons can also be indiscriminate in this way. Bombs and shells can fall outside of the intended target area to kill and maim people. Unexploded ordinance can lie about until triggered by someone. As such, chemical weapons do not seem to be necessarily worse than conventional weapons—rather it is the discrimination and persistence of the weapon that seem more important than the composition. For example, landmines certainly give chemical weapons strong competition in regards to being indiscriminate and persistent.

Thus, while a specific chemical weapon could be morally worse than a specific conventional weapon, chemical weapons are not inherently morally worse than conventional weapons.

Organizations to Contact

The editors have compiled the following list of organizations concerned with the issues debated in this book. The descriptions are derived from materials provided by the organizations. All have publications or information available for interested readers. The list was compiled on the date of publication of the present volume; the information provided here may change. Be aware that many organizations take several weeks or longer to respond to inquiries, so allow as much time as possible.

Arms Control Association (ACA)

1313 L St. NW, Suite 130, Washington, DC   20005

(202) 463-8270

website: www.armscontrol.org

The Arms Control Association (ACA) is a national nonpartisan membership organization dedicated to promoting public understanding of and support for effective arms control policies. Through its public education and media programs and its magazine, *Arms Control Today*, ACA provides policy makers, the press, and the interested public with authoritative information, analysis, and commentary on arms control proposals, negotiations, agreements, and related national security issues. In addition to the regular press briefings ACA holds on major arms control developments, the Association's staff provides commentary and analysis on a broad spectrum of issues for journalists and scholars both in the United States and abroad.

Australia Group (AG)

website: www.australiagroup.net

The Australia Group (AG) is an informal forum of countries seeking to ensure that exports do not contribute to the development of chemical or biological weapons (CBW). Coordination of national export control measures assists AG participants to fulfill their obligations under the Chemical Weapons Convention and the Biological and Toxin Weapons Convention to the fullest extent possible. AG participants encourage all countries to take the necessary steps to ensure that they and their industries are not contributing to the spread of CBW. The membership list and AG publications are among the documents that can be found on the AG website.

Centers for Disease Control and Prevention (CDC)

1600 Clifton Rd., Atlanta, GA   30333
(800) 232-4636
website: www.cdc.gov

The Centers for Disease Control and Prevention (CDC) works to protect the United States from health, safety, and security threats. As the US health protection agency, the CDC saves lives and protects people from health threats. To accomplish this mission, the CDC conducts critical research and provides health information to members of the health-care and public-safety community. The CDC's website includes a section devoted to emergency preparedness for bioterrorism, chemical emergencies, and radiation emergencies.

Federal Emergency Management Agency (FEMA)

500 C St. SW, Washington, DC   20472
(800) 621-3362
website: www.fema.gov

The Federal Emergency Management Agency (FEMA) is part of the US Department of Homeland Security. FEMA's mission is to support US citizens and first responders to ensure that as a nation the United States works together to build, sustain, and improve the capability to prepare for, protect against, respond to, recover from, and mitigate all hazards. In addition to information on disaster preparedness, mitigation, response, and recovery, the agency's website also contains FEMA's news releases along with a blog, videos, and photos.

Green Cross International (GCI)

9-11, rue de Varembé, Geneva   1202
  Switzerland
+41 22 789 16 62 • fax: +41 22 789 16 95
e-mail: gcinternational@gci.ch
website: www.gcint.org

The mission of Green Cross International (GCI) is to respond to the combined challenges of security, poverty, and environmental degradation to ensure a sustainable and secure future. To achieve this, GCI promotes legal, ethical, and behavioral norms to ensure basic changes in the values, actions, and attitudes of government, the private sector, and civil society; contributes to the prevention and resolution of conflicts arising from environmental degradation; and provides assistance to people affected by the environmental consequences of wars, conflicts, and man-made calamities. Information on GCI programs and events as well as press releases are available on its website.

Institute for Defence Studies and Analyses (IDSA)

1, Development Enclave, Rao Tula Ram Marg
New Delhi   110 010
  India
+91 11 2671 7983 • fax: +91 11 2615 4191
e-mail: contact.idsa@nic.in
website: www.idsa.in

The Institute for Defence Studies and Analyses (IDSA) is a nonpartisan, autonomous body dedicated to objective research and policy-relevant studies on all aspects of defence and security. Its mission is to promote national and international security through the generation and dissemination of knowledge on defence and security-related issues. Its website includes links to *CBW Magazine* and the *Journal of Defence Studies*.

International Institute for Counter-Terrorism (ICT)

Interdisciplinary Center (IDC) Herzliya, PO Box 167
Herzliya   4610101
  Israel
+972 9 9527277
e-mail: ict@idc.ac.il
website: www.ict.org.il

The International Institute for Counter-Terrorism (ICT) is working to develop innovative public policy on global terror through applied research on the phenomenon of terror and methods of coping with it. ICT aims to research the psychological aspects of counter-terrorism and to formulate recommendations to reduce the efficacy of the strategy of terror and improve the public's ability to endure this phenomenon. Since its establishment, ICT's activities have focused on academic-applied research, conferences and seminars, consulting services for decisionmakers, public diplomacy and educational activities, discussion and brainstorming forums, and building and maintaining databases. The Institute's website includes special reports and commentary on news items.

James Martin Center for Nonproliferation Studies (CNS)

460 Pierce St., Monterey, CA   93940
(831) 647-4154 • fax: (831) 647-3519
e-mail: cns@miis.edu
website: www.nonproliferation.org

The James Martin Center for Nonproliferation Studies (CNS) combats the spread of weapons of mass destruction by training the next generation of nonproliferation specialists and disseminating timely information and analysis. Many members of the Center's staff serve as expert advisers to policy makers on nonproliferation issues. CNS also holds seminars featuring decisionmakers and analysts in the field to provide a rich learning experience for students and staff alike. The Center's website includes information on the research programs, including the Chemical and Biological Weapons Nonproliferation Program, and publications, including *The Nonproliferation Review*.

Organisation for the Prohibition of Chemical Weapons (OPCW)

Johan de Wittlaan 32, The Hague   2517 JR
  The Netherlands
+31 70 416 3300 • fax: +31 70 306 3535
e-mail: media@opcw.org
website: www.opcw.org

The Organisation for the Prohibition of Chemical Weapons (OPCW) is an independent, autonomous, international organization with a working relationship with the United Nations. OPCW serves as the implementing body of the Chemical Weapons Convention (CWC), which entered into force in 1997. As of today, the OPCW has 190 member states, who are working together to achieve a world free from chemical weapons. They share the collective goal of preventing chemistry from ever again being used for warfare, thereby strengthening international security. To this end, the CWC contains four key provisions: destroying all existing chemical weapons under international verification by the OPCW; monitoring the chemical industry to prevent new weapons from re-emerging; providing assistance and protection to states parties against chemical threats; and fostering international cooperation to strengthen implementation of the CWC and promote the peaceful use of chemistry. The OPCW website contains links to recent publications and current news.

Pacific Northwest National Laboratory (PNNL)
Center for Global Security (CGS)

PO Box 999, Richland, WA   99352
(888) 375-7665
website: http://cgs.pnnl.gov

The Pacific Northwest National Laboratory's (PNNL) Center for Global Security (CGS) catalyzes the development of leading-edge national solutions to emerging issues, integrating science and technology, policy, and implementation expertise from across the global security community. Activities include interdisciplinary workshops, invited senior-level speakers, and a variety of analytical products. The Center is aligned with the National Security Directorate, which together focus on delivering high-impact, science-based, practical solutions to prevent and counter acts of terrorism and the proliferation of weapons of mass destruction. The Center's publications and information on current research projects is available on its website.

UPMC Center for Health Security
621 E Pratt St., Suite 210, Baltimore, MD   21202
(443) 573-3304 • fax: (443) 573-3305
website: www.upmchealthsecurity.org

The UPMC Center for Health Security works to protect the public's health from the consequences of epidemics and disasters and to ensure that communities are resilient to major challenges. One important area of focus for the Center is identifying, analyzing, and informing leaders about new and emerging biological, chemical, and nuclear accidents and intentional threats. The Center conducts independent research and analysis and communicates the results to inform the work of decisionmakers across communities. Copies of the Center's publications are available on its website.

Bibliography

Books

Ken Adelman   *Reagan at Reykjavik: Forty-Eight Hours That Ended the Cold War.* New York: Broadside Books, 2014.

Donald H. Avery   *Pathogens for War: Biological Weapons, Canadian Life Scientists, and North American Biodefense.* Toronto: University of Toronto Press, 2013.

Hans Blix   *Weapons of Terror: Freeing the World of Nuclear, Biological and Chemical Arms.* New York: United Nations, 2006.

Howard Blum   *Dark Invasion, 1915: Germany's Secret War and the Hunt for the First Terrorist Cell in America.* New York: Harper, 2014.

William R. Clark   *Bracing for Armageddon? The Science and Politics of Bioterrorism in America.* Oxford, United Kingdom: Oxford University Press, 2008.

Rosie Garthwaite   *How to Avoid Being Killed in a War Zone.* New York: Bloomsbury, 2011.

Jeanne Guillemin   *Biological Weapons: From the Invention of State-Sponsored Programs to Contemporary Bioterrorism.* New York: Columbia University Press, 2005.

| Kendall Hoyt | *Long Shot: Vaccines for National Defense*. Boston: Harvard University Press, 2012. |

| Annie Jacobsen | *Operation Paperclip: The Secret Intelligence Program That Brought Nazi Scientists to America*. Boston: Little, Brown and Company, 2014. |

| Gregory D. Koblentz | *Living Weapons: Biological Warfare and International Security*. Ithaca, NY: Cornell University Press, 2011. |

| Ulrich Krotz | *Flying Tiger: International Relations Theory and the Politics of Advanced Weapons*. Oxford, United Kingdom: Oxford University Press, 2011. |

| Milton Leitenberg, Raymond A. Zilinskas, and Jens H. Kuhn | *The Soviet Biological Weapons Program: A History*. Boston: Harvard University Press, 2012. |

| Vil S. Mirzayanov | *State Secrets: An Insider's Chronicle of the Russian Chemical Weapons Program*. Denver, CO: Outskirts Press, 2008. |

| National Research Council | *Remediation of Buried Chemical Warfare Materiel*. Washington, DC: The National Academies Press, 2012. |

| Richard M. Price | *The Chemical Weapons Taboo*. Ithaca, NY: Cornell University Press, 2007. |

| Edward M. Spiers | *A History of Chemical and Biological Weapons*. London: Reaktion Books, 2010. |

Jonathan B. Tucker	*War of Nerves: Chemical Warfare from World War I to al-Qaeda.* New York: Pantheon Books, 2006.

Periodicals and Internet Sources

Lauren Barbato	"Should the Last Smallpox Vials in the World Be Destroyed?" *Bustle,* May 5, 2014. www.bustle.com.
Nicholas Blanford	"Chlorine Attacks Sink Syria's Credibility on Chemical Weapons Deal," *Christian Science Monitor,* April 28, 2014.
Chad Boutin	"Nanotube-Infused Clothing May Protect Against Chemical Weapons," Phys.org, May 7, 2014. http://phys.org.
Steve Burgin	"WLKY Investigates: Toxic Neighbors," WLKY, February 5, 2013. www.wlky.com.
David Conde	"War Is Not What It Used to Be," *La Voz Colorado,* May 5, 2014. www.lavozcolorado.com.
Patrick Di Justo	"How to Destroy a Stockpile of Chemical Weapons," *New Yorker,* November 13, 2013.
Rick Gladstone	"Claims of Chlorine-Filled Bombs Overshadow Progress by Syria on Chemical Weapons," *New York Times,* April 22, 2014.

Frank Gottron and Dana A. Shea — "Federal Efforts to Address the Threat of Bioterrorism: Selected Issues and Options for Congress," Federation of American Scientists, February 8, 2011. www.fas.org.

Josh Lewis — "Are Chemical Weapons More Evil than Bullets & Bombs?," CNN, August 28, 2013. www.cnn.com.

He Na and Han Junhong — "Hidden Dangers, Ruined Lives," *China Daily*, May 15, 2014. http://usa.chinadaily.com.cn.

Steve Osunsami — "Living in Fear Near Chemical Weapons," ABC News, February 18, 2014. www.abcnews.go.com.

Peter Pringle — "Marcus Klingberg: The Spy Who Knew Too Much," *The Guardian*, April 26, 2014.

Martin Robbins — "Are Chemical Weapons Actually Useful in a War?," *Vice*, September 6, 2013. www.vice.com.

Alex Rogers — "Lawmakers Mull Biological Weapons Threat from Russia," *Time*, May 8, 2014.

Kent Sepkowitz — "Sarin, Nitrogen Mustard, Cyanide & More: All About Chemical Weapons," Daily Beast, August 26, 2013. www.thedailybeast.com.

Tess VandenDolder — "6 Evil Dictators Who Have Used Chemical Weapons," *In the Capital*, September 5, 2013. http://inthecapital .streetwise.co.

Voice of Russia — "Russia Destroys 80% of Its Chemical Weapons," May 12, 2014. http://voiceofrussia.com.

Bryan L. Williams and Melina S. Magsumbol — "Emergency Preparedness Among People Living Near US Army Chemical Weapons Sites After September 11, 2001," *American Journal of Public Health*, September 2007.

David Zucchino — "Deadly Chemical Weapons, Buried and Lost, Lurk Under U.S. Soil," *Los Angeles Times*, March 21, 2014.

Index

biotechnology concerns,
37–39

clear and present danger
from, 35–37

decreased funding for, 33–45

global health security, 44–45

ignorance over, 39–40

increased funding for, 28–32

overview, 21–22, 28–29, 33–35

potential consequences, 21–27

potential of, 24–25

testing of bioagents, 22–24

US food supply and, 46–57

See also Agroterrorism

Bird (avian) flu (H5N1), 34, 35,
37

Blackwell, Tom, 93–98

Blair, Charles, 94, 96, 97

Blue Grass Chemical Agent-
Destruction Pilot Plant, 7–9, 74,
76

Botulinum bacterium
(Clostridium botulinum), 82

Botulinum toxin, 82

Braun, Jane, 36

Brown, Stan, 96

Burr, Richard, 30

Bush, George H. W., 90

Bush, George W., 91

Bustani, José, 89

C

Cameron, Gavin, 96

Center for Arms Control & Non-
Proliferation, 98

Center for Biosecurity, 39

Centers for Disease Control and
Prevention (CDC), 7, 26, 36, 39

Central Intelligence Agency (CIA),
35, 81, 83–85

Chemical, biological, radiological
and nuclear (CBRN) threats, 13

Chemical and Biological Weapons
Nonproliferation Program, 68–69

Chemical warfare (CW)/weapons
future concerns over, 96–98
introduction, 7–9
material dumping, 9
not worse than conventional
weapons, 99–102
overview, 93–94
uniqueness of, 94–96
worse than conventional
weapons, 93–98
See also Biological weapons
(BW)/warfare; Israeli chemical weapons; Syrian chemical
weapons; United States (US)
chemical weapons destruc-
tion; Weapons of mass de-
struction; specific chemicals

Chemical Weapons Convention
(CWC), 64, 81, 86, 89, 96

Chengmin, Jin, 8

China, 23, 44

China Daily (newspaper), 8

Chlorine gas, 95–96

Clapper, James, 61

Clinton, Bill, 91

Clinton, Hillary Rodham, 35–36

Cluster weapons, 77–78, 93

Cohen, Avner, 84

Cold War, 22, 23, 29

Coll, Steve, 12

Commission on the Prevention of
WMD Proliferation and Terrorism, 26

Congressional Research Service, 27

US Department of Homeland Se-
curity, 49
US Environmental Protection
Agency, 8
US Food and Drug Administra-
tion (FDA), 39
US Justice Department, 66
US Office of Public Health Emer-
gency Preparedness, 33–34

V

Vanderbilt Institute for Integrative
Biosystems Research and Educa-
tion (VIIBRE), 20
Vanderbilt University, 19–20
Vanunu, Mordechai, 79, 80, 82
Vietnam, 65

W

War Powers Resolution, 67
Washington Post (newspaper), 12
Weaponization of pathogens, 17
Weapons of mass destruction
(WMD)
condemnation of, 97
effects of, 13
Israel and WMD agreements,
81–83

overview, 11–12
in Syria, 58–62
Weapons of Mass Destruction
Terrorism Research Center, 37
White phosphorous, 82
WikiLeaks, 80
Wiksow, John P., 10–20
Wolf in Sheep's Clothing modifi-
cation, 14–15
Wong, Kristina, 68–72
Woodrow Wilson School of Public
and International Affairs, 35
World War I, 8, 9, 47, 90
World War II, 8, 23

Y

Yale University School of Medi-
cine, 41
Yeltsin, Boris, 25
Yom Kippur war, 84

Z

Zakaria, Fareed, 60
Zarif, Javad, 60–61
Zilinskas, Raymond, 68–70
Zucchino, David, 7–8
Zunes, Stephen, 88–92